Colorado at Your Own Pace
Traveling by Motorhome with Friends

Also by Bernice Beard
At Your Own Pace: Traveling Your *Way in Your Motorhome*
Alaska at Your Own Pace: Traveling by RV Caravan

Colorado
At Your
Own Pace

Traveling by Motorhome with Friends

BERNICE BEARD

ARBOR HOUSE PUBLISHING
WESTMINSTER, MARYLAND

Every effort has been made to properly identify and capitalize trademark names used in this book. Pressman Toy Corporation is the owner worldwide of the trade name Rummikub®. Holiday Rambler® is a registered trademark of Monaco Coach Corporation. Winchester is a trademark of Olin Corporation and is used by permission. Colt is used with permission of Colt's Manufacturing Company, Inc. Honda and Accord are registered trademarks of American Honda Motor Co., Inc. The company's seven-step procedure for towing a vehicle behind a motorhome is as follows: 1. Check to be sure the transmission fluid level is full. 2. Release the parking brake. 3. Start the engine. 4. Shift the transmission from Park to Drive. 5. Shift from Drive to Neutral. 6. Turn off the engine; leave the key in the Accessory (1) position. 7. Make sure the radio and all accessories are turned off.

Grateful acknowledgment is made to Pressman Toy Corporation for permission to refer to Rummikub® in the manuscript and to John C. Graybeal for permission to use his photographs on pages 69, 97, 114, and 120.

Arbor House Publishing
332 One Forty Village Rd., Suite 7-197
Westminster, MD 21157
(410) 857-4146; (800) 966-4146; Fax: (410) 857-3835

Ordering Information

Quantity sales. Special discounts are available on quantity purchases by corporations, associations, and others. For details, contact the "Special Sales Department" at the Arbor House Publishing address above.

Printed in the United States of America

Library of Congress Cataloging-in-Publication Data
Beard, Bernice, 1927–
    Colorado at your own pace: traveling by motorhome with friends / by Bernice Beard
1st ed   p. cm.
Includes appendix and index.
International Standard Book Number: 0-9653063-7-2.
    1. Beard, Bernice, 1927—Journeys, Colorado
    2. Colorado—Description and travel
    3. Recreational vehicles—United States
    4. Motorhomes—United States
    5. Voyages and travels
917.880433-dc21 1999
Library of Congress Catalog Card Number: 98-094838
CIP First Edition

Cover Design: Robert Aulicino, Pro-Art Graphic Design
Interior Design: Marin Bookworks
Cover Photographs: Inset: Pikes Peak by © Ernie Ferguson; Full page: Garden of the Gods by © 1998 David O. Bailey
Cover Motorhome: Holiday Rambler® Presidential
Editorial Services: PeopleSpeak

The author and publisher assume neither liability nor responsibility to any person or entity with respect to any direct or indirect loss or damage caused, or alleged to be caused, by the information contained herein, or for errors, omissions, inaccuracies, or any other inconsistency within these pages, or for unintentional slights against people or organizations. The author and publisher are not associated with any manufacturers of motorhomes (or other products) and are not guaranteeing the safety of these homes.

Distributed by: Seven Hills Book Distributors, Cincinnati, OH, (800) 545-2005

To

John and Lib Graybeal

in thankfulness for

their friendship, leadership,

and all-around good fun and spirit

as we traveled together from Maryland to Colorado

and home again

and to Paul,

for his love, positive outlook,

wisdom, determination in solving problems,

and exemplary driving in unexpected circumstances.

Contents

Preface

COMBINE THE ATTRACTIONS (museums and mountains, cities and cliff dwellings, hot springs and ski slopes, gorges and cattle ranches) of Colorado with a love of traveling by motorhome and a passion for writing that helps others enjoy and understand the recreational vehicle (RV) lifestyle, and you have the reason for this work.

Whether you're new to motorhoming, a veteran RVer, or an armchair traveler, these pages were written to transport you on a 25-day motorhome journey from Maryland to Colorado. They give you an insider's view as they let you in on the planning, happenings, and allurements en route.

The detail and clarity of the technical information benefits both seasoned and new RVers. The index is a valuable aid in finding the information you need. The appendix offers a travel checklist as well as lists of membership benefit card sources, campground and truck-center directories, presidential libraries, National Park System sites in the Colorado area, and a useful glossary of RV terms.

Our adventure in Colorado and the subsequent writing of this book began with a simple invitation one fall from our friends John and Elizabeth "Lib" Graybeal. They asked if my husband, Paul, and I would like to caravan with them on a motorhome trek to Colorado the following spring.

At first I wasn't certain I wanted to go on the trip. I questioned how a 25-day journey to Colorado could top the previous 44-day, 12-RV caravan tour to Alaska that the four of us had enjoyed. What could possibly outdo that? I asked myself. The Alaska trip was a once-in-a-lifetime experience. I decided I had to reset my expectation gauge and come down to earth.

We accepted John and Lib's gracious invitation, having had good times on the road with them before. Like the motorhome travel veterans that we were, the four of us started our westward journey with high spirits, a certain savoir-faire, and faith in the Almighty. I'm thrilled that we went.

As is my natural bent when traveling on a long journey, I made handwritten notes in a trip log and a spiral-bound tablet. Both of these lay within easy reach of the passenger seat in our motorhome. Having become comfortable with using a laptop computer en route, I used the device almost every day to enter notes about our travels. It was fun to have it on my lap, look at the countryside, and almost effortlessly type in what I saw, thought, or felt. Along the way, I also collected receipts, leaflets, brochures, and newspapers. I took pictures with an automatic camera, making handwritten notes of the date, time, subject, and other pertinent comments on the spot in a small, handy spiral notebook that fit in my pocket.

As we traveled, we referred to the *Trailer Life Directory for Campgrounds, RV Parks & Services* for ideas on where to stay, to AAA maps and booklets for travel directions and sightseeing information, and to maps and brochures that we collected at welcome centers for the individual states we visited. I cannot emphasize enough how helpful each of these sources is for travelers.

In addition to the information in the book you have in your hand, I would encourage travelers to Colorado (or anywhere) to take with them a campground directory and a set of AAA or other travel reference guides and to stop at welcome centers for more detailed information about their travel destinations.

I have many persons to thank for their part in the joyful labor of this book. Paul provided valuable technical information on the road and in these pages. He is intrigued by and enjoys learning about electronics, mechanics, and other technical subjects. Before retiring after 38 years on the job, he worked with long-distance and specialized circuits for the Chesapeake and Potomac Telephone Company of Maryland (later Bell Atlantic-MD).

I thank with a deeply grateful heart Lib and John Graybeal, our gracious fellow travelers, for being a vital, congenial part of these pages and for kindly wading through the manuscript in the editing stage, providing memories, details, and photographs that add to the accuracy and enjoyment of the book.

I acknowledge with heartfelt appreciation the help of the following persons: Nancy Beard, my astute daughter-in-law who owns Creative CAD and Graphics, for designing the delightful drawings on the page headings—ones that served so well for my first two books; Joel Friedlander of Marin Bookworks, for his inviting interior design; Jane Sharpe, for her expert library-cataloging copy; Robert Aulicino, Pro-Art Graphic Design, for designing the appealing and irresistible cover; Rachel Rice, for her usual excellent indexing; and Sharon Goldinger of PeopleSpeak, the editor who makes sure readers have the details they need for a clear image of what's happening and for her overall good spirit and expertise.

A very special thank you to readers who have told me they enjoyed my first two books, *At Your Own Pace: Traveling Your Way in Your Motorhome* and *Alaska at Your Own Pace: Traveling by RV Caravan*. These include fellow members of the Westminster Church of the Brethren and its camping group, the Western Maryland College community, and other friends and family nearby and far away, all of whom continue to inspire and encourage me and whose friendship Paul and I treasure.

In closing, my aim is for these pages to bring you reading pleasure, give you insights into RVing by showing you motorhoming from the inside out, demonstrate for you how two couples in two motorhomes can travel together, excite and educate you about Colorado, and in the appendix provide you with additional information on national parks and presidential libraries for your own travels.

This book will show that you, too, can tour Colorado at *your* own pace. For the moment, however, just ride along with us as we enter springtime in the Rockies.

About the Author

Bernice Beard is a published writer of essays, articles, short stories, and books. In addition to writing, she is an active member of the Church of the Brethren. In 1989 she retired after a 27-year career in administration at Western Maryland College, a private liberal arts college, as executive assistant to the president emerita. She holds a bachelor of arts and master of liberal arts degrees from that same institution. Her favorite activities include writing, walking, and of course, traveling by motorhome.

She lives near Westminster, Maryland, with her husband, Paul. They have a son, Jeffrey, and a daughter-in-law, Nancy. The author and her husband have taken 15 major trips in their motorhome, including the 25-day RV journey to Colorado about which she writes in this book.

She is listed in *Who's Who of American Women* and was awarded a Special Achievement Award by Western Maryland College for her first book, *At Your Own Pace: Traveling Your Way in Your Motorhome.*

1

The Invitation
and Preparation

MY HUSBAND, PAUL, a modern-day
Renaissance man, appeared noncommittal when he told me that our
friends John and Elizabeth "Lib" Graybeal had asked if we would like
to caravan with them on a motorhome odyssey to Colorado the following late May and early June.

While traveling in the motorhome is Paul's lifetime dream and his
absolute favorite venture, he enjoys refining our eight-year-old recreational vehicle (RV) so that it grows more comfortable to inhabit, convenient to operate and maintain, and powerful. He is always busy
readying the rig for the next journey. Not full-timers (people who live
permanently in their RVs), we enjoy taking frequent trips by
motorhome, both on weekends with our local camping group and for
longer stretches by ourselves or with others.

"Colorado?" I asked. "Why Colorado?"

"John said that Lib has never seen it. He also wants to perhaps
visit presidential sites on the way out or back."

My mind shifted into high gear as it searched for answers as to
why _we_ would want to go to Colorado. We had, after all, been there
at least twice already, although I did have to admit it was to only the
eastern part around Denver. Mostly, my thoughts raced back and
forth between Colorado and Alaska. I questioned whether a three-
week trip to Colorado could possibly match the spectacular three-
month journey the four of us had previously taken to Alaska.
(Coloradans, please forgive my naivete!)

Two years earlier we had traveled in tandem with the Graybeals as our two motorhomes crossed the United States to Vancouver, British Columbia, where the four of us joined a recreational vehicle caravan tour—destination, Alaska. Following a 44-day tour of British Columbia, the Yukon, and Alaska, the Graybeals returned to Maryland by the most direct route. Meanwhile, Paul and I leisurely visited relatives and friends in the western states on our way back to our home in Maryland. The Colorado trip could be our first complete trip with John and Lib.

I must be overlooking something that excites others about the state of Colorado, I thought. I liked the notion of visiting presidential libraries and museums along the way and considered the possibility that there were spectacular sights and interesting places in Colorado that I had never seen and didn't know about.

"Do *you* want to go?" I asked Paul, thinking that after one of his often lengthy, well-thought-out sentences that delved into all aspects of a question, he would end up saying no.

"Yes," he said. "It's a good opportunity to really see the state. I know that sights such as the Royal Gorge exist, but I don't know what they are really like. I think you would enjoy the trip also."

I was surprised! Quickly, my imagination began dancing with Paul's vision. Royal Gorge was appealing to him, he said, but it was a place I didn't know existed. I began to wonder what we had missed seeing on our previous visits. Although I had ridden in a car to the top of Mount Evans near Denver, I had never seen the famous Pikes Peak that other friends had talked about. Knowing that Colorado was a favorite travel destination for many people, I sensed it must offer many other exciting scenes and activities. Besides, if our friends the Graybeals, who were inveterate travelers, planned to go, surely they felt the trip was worthwhile.

From somewhere in my distant, countrified past, I saw and heard a smiling cowboy in the movies strumming his guitar and singing, "When it's springtime in the Rockies . . . I'll be coming back to you." I felt an irresistible pull toward the west.

During the eight years that we had owned our 34-foot, Holiday Rambler® motorhome, I loved stepping up into its many-windowed, homelike interior; feeling the thrill of being in a world of freedom, independence, and adventure; and heading out wherever we chose to go. And I loved having the comforts of home with us as we traveled.

Based on my passion for traveling in the motorhome and Paul's eagerness—and realizing that my vision and knowledge of Colorado were limited and that the zest for the destination would come in time—we decided to go on the trip.

The Graybeals and we attended the same church, belonged to the same church camping group, and worked on church projects together. Lib and I had known each other and been friends for many years. We had attended the same New Windsor High School (she graduated the year after I did). Her family's dairy farm and my grand-parents' small farm were adjacent to one another.

We had had a great time with John and Lib during our Alaskan jaunt. On that journey, the caravan tour company planned almost everything. We caravaners simply followed instructions and route directions from the "wagonmasters." Any problems with our vehicles were tended to by the "tailgunners." For the Colorado trip, however, our foursome would decide where to go, what to do, where to camp, whether to eat in or out, and what time to leave in the mornings.

The Colorado trip was actually John's brainchild. When a brief note from him came in late December by U.S. mail, it piqued my interest. In it he gave "just a couple of thoughts" on the upcoming trip. He suggested visiting the Truman Library in Independence, Missouri; the Eisenhower Center and Dodge City in Kansas; and in Colorado, Pueblo, Canon City, Cripple Creek, Durango, Mesa Verde, Boulder, Denver, Pikes Peak, Colorado Springs, and the Air Force Academy.

He also said that we might want to return home in time for the June campout of our church camping group, that we should proba-bly allow around three and one-half to four weeks for the trip, and to feel free to offer ideas.

About a month before our departure, John mailed to us what he called a "rough/suggested itinerary." It read as follows:

Leave week of May 15—after Mother's Day.

Basically [go] out I-70; could detour second day for lunch with friends near Wilmington, OH.

Stops at Independence, MO, and Abilene, KS, for presidents.

At Salina, KS, head south to McPherson, then southwest to Dodge City. From Dodge City, stay on U.S. 50 to Pueblo, CO. Somewhere in that area, pick a campground for several days while we visit:

Colorado Springs

Air Force Academy

Canon City

Royal Gorge

Cripple Creek

Pikes Peak

Then west and south or south and west to Durango and Mesa Verde National Park. Then work our way back north and east to Denver with some side trips worked in. Sightsee Denver and any other notable attractions.

Instead of the interstate back, perhaps take U.S. 36 across northern Kansas and Missouri to Hannibal, and then on to Springfield, IL (another president).

Arrive back home the week before we camp at Safari— like the 10th to 12th of June.

Just a general plan subject to change, modifications, deletions, additions, and any other adjectives you can think of.

P.S. We'll tow a car; that'll equalize the gas mileage somewhat. [John and Lib's motorhome got better gas mileage than ours.]

By the time we got John's December "rough/suggested itinerary" letter, I had examined maps, read tour books, and talked with people about Colorado, so I had a much better idea of what I wanted to see and do when we toured that state. Paul and I both liked John's itinerary.

When I looked closely at Colorado's state boundaries on a map, I realized that they form an almost perfect rectangle. Pikes Peak is in its center with the Rocky Mountains extending from north to south in the central third of the state. To my surprise, six major rivers originate in Colorado's mountains—the South and North Platte Rivers, the Republican, the Colorado, the Arkansas, and the Rio Grande.

I had not realized that the eastern part of the state is a huge plain, mostly level but with high elevations of 3,000 feet or more. Covering about a third of the state, the plain is backed by the majestic Rocky Mountains in the central third and the Colorado Plateau in the western third. Mesas, valleys, and deep canyons characterize the plateau region.

I searched for information about Colorado from the library, my computer encyclopedia, and old tour books. I gleaned that the highest point in Colorado, and in fact in the entire Rocky Mountain range from western New Mexico through west-central Colorado and up into Canada (where it is known as the Canadian Rockies), is Mount Elbert at 14,433 feet, while the lowest is the Arkansas Valley at 3,350 feet above sea level. These high altitudes, I read, sometimes have a negative affect on the bodies of visitors not used to them—a note that I dismissed lightly.

Since higher elevations generally have more precipitation, and since Colorado contains 53 of the nation's 80 peaks over 14,000 feet, the state looks to its snowpacked Rocky Mountains for much of its water supply.

I eagerly discovered that Colorado's history dates back 20,000 years to nomadic hunters and includes the cliff dwellers who lived at Mesa Verde by A.D. 800. The area's early explorers were Spanish—the first was probably Francisco Coronado in 1541. The Louisiana Purchase in 1803 included the eastern and central parts of Colorado. The remainder of the state changed from Spanish to Mexican rule and became part of the United States under the treaty that ended the

Mexican War in 1848. Colorado became our 38th state on August 1, 1876.

Colorado's economy is supported by manufacturing, agriculture, tourism, and mining. One fact that surprised me was that Colorado needs the runoff water from the snowcapped Rocky Mountains to help irrigate its semiarid eastern plains—its climate is relatively dry.

Colorado's major cities are Denver, the state capital; Greeley; Boulder; Colorado Springs; Pueblo; and Grand Junction. The state's population is about 3.5 million, most of whom live in urban areas. When I learned that, I knew that we would probably travel through some areas with few houses and people. I love to see isolated countryside and mountains. It makes me aware of my own identity and being.

To me, the name Colorado had a wide-ranging, enticing ring. From a dictionary I discovered that in addition to the state, the name had been attached to a blue spruce tree, a college, two rivers, a desert, a plateau, a potato beetle, a red cedar tree, a city with nearby mineral springs, and a tick fever.

Eventually, I learned that "colorado" is Spanish for "colored" or "reddish" and that William Gilpin, the first territorial governor, chose that name in 1861 because the region contained the source of the reddish-colored Colorado River. I began to sense that the state contained overwhelmingly more to see and do than we could possibly fit into the two weeks that we planned to stay there.

We had other plans in addition to sightseeing. Paul and I had learned that Paul's sister Hazel Guyer and her husband, Al, who live in Pennsylvania, would be in the mountains south of Denver during the time of our trip. They would be camp co-managers for a Church of the Brethren outdoor facility called Camp Colorado. Paul and I hoped to include a visit to the Guyers in the itinerary.

None of us had any idea what kind of weather or perilous adventures the excursion would include. Yet we should have suspected possible risks when people asked us, "Why are you going to Colorado so early in the year?"

"We want to go before schools are out. And that's the time that John and Lib had in their minds. It suits us, too," I said, holding steadfastly to the appeal of "When It's Springtime in the Rockies" and picturing blooming wildflowers in wooded mountains.

Later, for various reasons, we all agreed to start out on Wednesday, May 17, which happened to be Paul's birthday. Our planning as far as specific campgrounds and sights to see remained low key—we had no written itinerary for each day's travel.

During the month before we left, Paul did his usual careful check and maintenance of the motorhome before a major trip. He looked at the record book he kept for the motorhome and decided that it was time for an oil change. Even though the recommended 3,000 miles had not quite been reached, he went ahead and changed the oil and filter so we wouldn't have to do it during our trip.

He also took the time to do the following from his checklist:

Check on gasoline for motorhome
Check on propane gas
Obtain supply of oil for motorhome engine
Lubricate chassis
Change transmission oil and filter and refill, if necessary
    [It was not quite necessary, but he did it anyway.]
Check auxiliary generator to be sure it operates and
    check oil level and change as noted in manual
Check front wheel bearings and brake pads
Check radiator
Check furnace to be sure it works properly
Check water heater to be sure it works properly
Check tires (spare also)
Check all lights outside and inside to be sure they work
Check batteries
Take along any additional specialty tools that might be
    needed
Take along books and literature that may be needed for
    maintenance or repair
Check power-steering fluid
Check brake fluid
Stop newspaper

Get cash in $20 bills

Make sure funds are in account for debit card

Pay ahead the following:

    house and car insurance

    gasoline service bill

    gas and electric bill

    telephone bill

    fuel oil bill

During his trip preparations, Paul commented to me that the tire treads on the motorhome were showing signs of wear and all eight tires would need replacing soon, but they should be fine for summer travel. Since we didn't anticipate running into snow, I was just as glad to postpone that expense. I would later recall that one fleeting moment of satisfaction and realize how unaware I had been of its ramifications.

Meanwhile, I followed my checklists, making sure we had on board supplies and equipment necessary for the trip. I set up a portable clothes rack in our bedroom on which we hung the clothes we planned to take with us. A table in the living room served as a depository for articles that would eventually go into the motorhome. Whenever we went past the table on our way outside to the motorhome, we took along whatever lay on top.

My checklist of items included the following:

Turn on refrigerator in RV a few days before leaving to be sure it works, to begin freezing ice cubes, and to load frozen foods.

Leave license plate number of RV with appropriate person.

Leave telephone numbers and addresses of stops en route with appropriate person.

Leave obituary file in obvious place and be sure appropriate person has a house key and knows location of important papers. [The obituary file contains our instructions in the event of death.]

> Make arrangements for mail: (1) Use mail forwarding ser-
> vice or (2) ask appropriate person to handle mail
> while we are away or (3) arrange with post office to
> forward or hold mail. [For the Colorado trip, I asked
> the post office to hold our mail until we returned.]
>
> Get maps and tour books as needed and place in passen-
> ger seat area.
>
> Call neighbors on either side of house to let them know
> our departure and return dates.
>
> Get groceries or load RV from what we have on hand.

As we prepare for a trip in our home's comfort and safety, it's so easy to assume the same conditions and weather and security will be with us wherever we go. We will cope if they are not, we tell ourselves. On the road, however, we're always glad we brought along galoshes and an umbrella or an extra pair of shoes when we encounter rain and muddy conditions. The best way to pack, we have found, is to prepare for whatever conditions we can imagine.

Following these checklists as well as an inventory-type checklist that appears in the appendix gives us a sense of inner peace and organization. At times in the past, thinking I was experienced enough not to need my checklists, I had tried preparing for a weekend trip without looking at the lists, but when I skimmed them at the last minute, I always discovered items that I needed or wanted to take with us.

As time for our departure to Colorado drew closer, I wondered what to plan for Paul's birthday, which would occur on the very first day of our trip with Lib and John. On the Saturday before we left, while Paul and our son, Jeff, attended an air show nearby, I baked an angel food cake to surprise Paul on his birthday. I called Lib to let her know, explaining that I didn't frost the cake because Paul did not like a lot of sugary sweet icing. Before Paul returned, I placed the cake in the freezer in our house to keep it fresh.

The following Tuesday, I secretly packed the frozen cake in a large cardboard box inside a huge, black plastic leaf bag, then placed the monstrosity into the motorhome's bathtub. I warned Paul not to touch it. I'm sure he guessed what was in it, but he played along anyway. At least he didn't know *everything* I planned for his birth-day. In fact, *I* didn't know exactly what my plans were, for they would depend on the circumstances at the time.

By Tuesday evening, we had loaded the motorhome with clothes for all kinds of weather. The refrigerator/freezer and pantry bulged. I always take foods that I know we like, often transferring items from my cupboards and freezer in the house plus doing some special shop-ping in my usual grocery store in order to stock up the motorhome. I knew we'd eat in restaurants along the way also. My homemade trip log, eight-by-five-inch spiral tablet, and laptop computer waited near the passenger seat for our impending departure. With Paul's birth-day cake on board and our plans to head out the next morning, my initial hesitation about going to Colorado was turning into a kind of waiting-for-Santa-Claus anticipation. To top it off, the house was clean and orderly, something that I had found from previous trips would be an inviting "welcome home."

2

On-the-Road Birthday Party

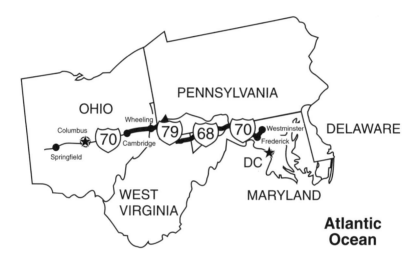

IT WAS PAUL'S 69th birthday—Wednesday, May 17—the very day we would head out on a three-week excursion to Colorado with our friends the Graybeals. As I ate my usual breakfast in the yellow kitchen of our story-and-a-half Cape Cod–style home, I wondered how Paul's birthday celebration would work out that evening. My plans involved using the Graybeals' tow car, but I hesitated to ask them about it. While I like to help other people, I am reluctant to ask others to help me.

"In about 10 minutes," I told John Graybeal over the telephone when he asked if we were ready for our Colorado excursion. The kitchen clock said 7:45 A.M. We had planned informally to meet about 8:30. It was good that Paul and I were up early and almost ready to go.

The Graybeals lived about 20 minutes from us, so John said they would leave in about five minutes and meet us at the end of our street.

"What channel should we use for the CB [citizen's band radio]?" he asked. "Eleven or 13?"

"I'm sure whatever you say is fine with us. Paul is outside cleaning the motorhome windshield."

"Well, let's make it 13 then." Since we were taking our new cellular telephone, I gave John the number to give to his son, Jay, who was John's liaison between home and the road.

If an all-seeing eye were looking, it would have observed me toting bed pillows, makeup, and a shopping bag with cereal and bread to the motorhome. Back in the house I made sure the electric heater dials in both bathrooms in the house were turned off, the television and computer were unplugged, and the windows were locked. I looked at all the electrical outlets in Paul's office on the first floor and saw that nothing was plugged into any of them. I had previously "trip-readied" my office on the second floor.

Earlier that morning Paul had locked the front and basement doors to the house. Having pushed a tiny lever into position, I felt the latch on the small garage door lock as I closed it behind me. After tugging on the doorknob a few times to be sure the lock was secure, I walked to the motorhome.

And so with a cold, somewhat snowy Maryland winter behind us, hazy skies above us, and the promise of bright sunshine in the springtime of Colorado ahead, Paul eased our 34-foot Holiday Rambler® motorhome out of our driveway and onto the hilly, two-lane, paved country road that runs in front of our modest house.

Whenever we pull our huge vehicle out of our driveway, crossing both lanes, we always try to find a significant break in traffic so that nobody has to wait as we swing back into our own lane of traffic. As usual, like mechanical robots, both of us looked both ways for oncoming traffic. From the passenger seat, I jotted down in my home-made trip log the essentials of the moment: Date: *Wednesday, May 17*; Time: *7:59 A.M.*; Odometer: *65,118*; Overnight Name and Location:

Lv. home driveway; Driver: *P*; Weather: *60 degrees, hazy, overcast, cloudy.*

Once safely on the road, exhilarated at being in the motorhome and once again on a trip, we headed to the end of our street, where we parked in a large, dirt-paved, vacant lot. The cloudy skies had begun to release a light drizzle. Soon John announced over the CB that they were passing West Main Street and then Meadow Branch Church. In a few minutes, we saw their 34-foot, Class A, Pinnacle motorhome in the distance.

It glided steadily on Route 140 toward us. Our CB radio crackled again. John invited Paul to take the lead. After a brief pause, Paul declined politely. He said he would prefer that John lead because of his keener eyesight.

The Graybeals slowly passed in front of us. Lib and I smiled broadly and waved gleefully to one another from our passenger seats. Paul pulled out behind them. Melding smoothly as if rehearsed, our two RVs headed north on the smooth, two-lane Route 140 toward Taneytown.

John and Lib's motorhome was cream colored with its brand name in small teal green letters on the front, sides, and rear. A band of green-and-black striping ran the length of its lower body on both sides and around the rear just below the name. Inside their large rear window hung a rose-colored, accordion-pleated blind. A black "sweeper" hung from the rear bumper to protect their tow car from dirt and stones thrown backward by the rear wheels of the motorhome. Their tow car was Lib's taupe Honda Accord station wagon. Paul and I would see the rear of their motorhome and tow car during much of the trip. At that moment we were following about 300 or 400 feet behind them.

"I really ought to be back from John at least a quarter of a mile," said Paul. "It gives room to maneuver in case he has to make a panic stop. Also it gives people passing us a chance to get in and out of this lane."

That amount of space between our motorhomes also gave us a broader view of the countryside than if we followed closely behind the Graybeals' vehicles.

John and Lib could see our 34-foot, Class A, Holiday Rambler® motorhome following them in their side view mirrors. It, too, was cream colored, but its bands of striping at the top, middle, and bottom of the vehicle were silver, blue, and red. Anyone following our vehicle could not see inside the rear window because Paul had blocked it off in order to get rid of a draft over the bed when he remodeled that room. And we, of course, did not take a tow car because John and Lib had graciously volunteered to take theirs.

Paul drove with our headlights on, which helped John to know where we were behind him.

Over the CB, Paul said that his navigator (me) thought we should use some identification when we talked on the CB other than the numbers we had used when we were part of the Alaskan caravan tour. Paul's CB "handle" already was Milkweed. He had chosen that name because it was a word that was distinctive when pronounced and easily recognized. Soon Lib came up with Chainsaw for John since he had been sawing a lot of wood on their property. My CB name was already Reindeer, which I had chosen because I liked the idea of Santa's reindeer pulling a sleigh full of presents. It had a fun, outdoor connotation. But although we tried and tried, we never could decide on a good handle for Lib.

Thus began our trip, at 8:11 A.M. in light drizzle, with Milkweed and Chainsaw driving and Lib and Reindeer riding in the navigator seats. I was prepared to drive as Paul's relief, but I knew he might want the satisfaction of having driven all the way himself. Lib could drive also if needed.

"You realize that my stenographer is taking notes, don't you?" I heard Paul say over the CB as he saw my head bent over the small, spiral-bound notebook that I kept handy beside me on the carpeted engine hump.

"I figured that out," said John as we glided toward Taneytown, just 10 miles from home.

By the time we reached the South Mountain Rest Area, off I-70, our windshield wipers swished steadily back and forth. In our years of motorhome travel, we had learned to take breaks whether that meant stopping at a rest area, taking a short walk, or simply having lunch. Both the body and mind suffer fatigue otherwise.

The rain continued spattering against our windshield as we headed west on I-70 until the highway turned north and we went westward on I-68 instead. About 11:30 A.M., we drove into the truck stop at Keysers Ridge, parking there while we ate lunch in our motorhomes. Rain that we had encountered most of the morning had stopped, but dark clouds drifted above us.

It was our first lunch stop. While I retrieved sliced ham and turkey, a loaf of bread, pickles, and margarine from the refrigerator and set the dinette table with paper plates and plastic tableware, Paul went outside to check the tires and generally see that all was in order on the motorhome.

By the time Paul re-entered our cozy quarters, the table was spread. We each fixed our own sandwiches according to our individual tastes, as we always did at home. We sat eating and looking out the large dinette window, watching trucks move in an out of the large parking area. Paul decided to eat his usual vanilla ice cream for dessert and he scooped a dip for me also. I reached behind me from the dinette seat, opened the refrigerator door, and pulled out from the interior door shelf my favorite topping—chocolate syrup. We didn't hurry as we cleared away our lunch plates. We had no dishes to wash; we usually keep china and silverware to a minimum at lunchtime so that we don't have to wash dishes during the day. That saves time that would be spent doing that task as well as liquefied propane (LP) gas for heating water and lets us get farther down the road.

After a leisurely half-hour, Paul climbed behind the wheel and I got into the passenger seat. We looked to our left and saw that John and Lib were in their respective places. Paul reached for the CB. "Shall we do it?" he asked John, who gave an affirmative reply.

Our two vehicles left the truck stop and regained I-68 heading toward Morgantown, West Virginia, 41 miles away. A strong wind rushed against our rigs. The sky was still dark, but it looked a little lighter.

I assumed we were driving through a rainy front and were on the western edge of it. Rolling mountains in the distance looked bright, and the road appeared to be getting drier.

White dogwood blossoms stood out among wooded hillsides. So far that morning, I had seen a blooming wisteria tree, locust trees, and a lacy, bloom-laden sycamore tree. Wine-colored young buds and shoots on deciduous trees gave them the subdued appearance of fall foliage.

I was planning to take my usual 10-minute nap after lunch, but Paul wanted me to help guide him through Morgantown, now 30 miles ahead.

A sign welcomed us to West Virginia and reminded us that the speed limit was 65 miles per hour. Both John and Paul preferred to drive about 55 for safety reasons as well as to cause less wear and tear on the vehicles and to get better gasoline mileage.

A great field of wild yellow buttercups blanketed a knoll along I-68. The scenic route healed the heart with spring-green mountain foliage and views of deep valleys, old roads, and lakes. These were the hills of West Virginia.

The dual highway looked dry. Our windshield wipers rested from their morning bout with rain and strong winds.

Except for the trip to Alaska with our caravanning group of 24, Paul and I were used to traveling alone. But a foursome was different and I couldn't help wondering how we would get along; what adjustments, efforts, and sacrifices we would each make; and whether we would have fun. I wouldn't call myself a fuddy-duddy; lately, I had come to place a lot of value on fun. Fun was healthy. Newspapers, magazines, and television health segments were reporting studies that showed the physical benefits of smiling and laughing, that these actions do indeed strengthen the body's immune system. Human interest stories told of how watching humorous television shows and movies helped ill patients to recuperate. Besides, I had always liked hearing jokes and telling them. My Uncle Sam and Uncle Tommy on my father's side of the family always had a new joke to tell me as a young girl when they visited us on the farm. These days my brother-in-law Ralph Taylor smiles and says, "Bernie, have you heard the one about . . . ?"

Although I had looked forward to this trip, I was not overly excited about it, which puzzled me. I hoped I was not taking for granted our good fortune in being able to travel during our retirement. Perhaps my lack of zeal was because it had been less than three months since we returned from Florida, where we stayed in our motorhome for two and one-half winter months and did sightseeing on the Gulf Coast.

The most interesting part of the upcoming trip for me would be traveling with the Graybeals because I knew they took time to sightsee. When Paul and I traveled alone, he usually didn't care to sightsee, while I did. On this trip we planned stops at the homes and libraries of Presidents Harry S. Truman, Dwight D. Eisenhower, and Abraham Lincoln as well as Mark Twain. Then, too, I hoped to go up Pikes Peak and to see one of the famous Colorado ski resorts, such as Aspen or Vail. I was curious to see how Paul related to sightseeing. He seemed to enjoy it in Alaska; perhaps he needed the motivation of friends.

The trip interrupted the process of getting my first motorhoming book *(At Your Own Pace: Traveling Your Way in Your Motorhome)* published. But then I needed a break from it anyway. When covering as much distance as we planned on this trip, no time or energy remained for work projects other than journaling by writing and photography, so I did not bring the manuscript along. Instead, I brought a book about Christian writing, my Pentax® IQ Zoom 115 camera with print and slide film, audio cassette tapes from a Christian writers conference that I had recently attended, and my Bible.

As we continued toward Morgantown, I felt fairly rested and at peace riding along, looking at the scenery, and talking with Paul. He liked to drive. The sun shone, casting moving shadows on the highway ahead from trucks and cars as they passed.

West of Morgantown, we made the transition to I-79 heading for the town of Washington, Pennsylvania, and then regained I-70 as it headed westward once again. A sign welcomed us to Pennsylvania at 1:25 P.M. Another said "55 Miles Per Hour Speed Limit." On I-70, we crossed the narrow upper panhandle of West Virginia, and a little after three o'clock, we crossed the Ohio River and entered that state. The speed limit was 65 miles per hour.

That stretch of I-70 West was bumpy. I took a determined nap on the sofa about 2:15 and awakened feeling as if my head had been in a vibrator. The resulting headache sent me to the medicine cabinet for an acetaminophen capsule and to the gallon jug for water to take the pill.

Suddenly we saw signs about a detour to U.S. 40 West because of road construction. Just as suddenly, my excitement about the trip perked up as we drove onto a road we hadn't taken before. My sudden enthusiasm told me my earlier nonchalance came from having been to Ohio, Missouri, Kansas, and Colorado on previous journeys. At that point, I realized that each trip, whether or not I had visited the same territory earlier, begot its own new and exciting adventures. During the detour, we agreed over the CB to have dinner together to celebrate Paul's birthday that evening.

The detour took us to I-77. From there we regained I-70 and turned off at exit 178 to reach our first night's campground. As is customary, we stopped at the office of the campground, in this instance, Spring Valley Campground, Cambridge, Ohio. I retrieved from the glove compartment our membership cards for Paul to take along into the office. (See the appendix for a list of the cards we carry.) We kept the cards bound with a rubber band so they were handy whenever we registered at a campground. Spring Valley Campground was a Good Sampark, which meant that members of the Good Sam Club are given a 10 percent discount off the usual cost for a campsite. As members, we were eligible for the discount.

After registering, we and the Graybeals pulled into side-by-side campsites about 4:15 P.M. Warm air greeted me when I stepped outside to talk to Lib. Overcoming my reluctance to request a favor, I asked Lib and John about using the tow car to go out to dinner. Through their screen door, she and John suggested and I agreed that we take Paul to a nearby Bob Evans Restaurant at five o'clock for a birthday celebration. It was an easy arrangement after all. We seem to have similar interests and desires.

Meanwhile, Paul hooked up our motorhome to the campground's water and electricity, both simple tasks. For the water, he pulled the coiled water hose from the outside compartment located toward the rear of the motorhome on the driver's side, threaded one end of the hose to the receiver at the motorhome, and attached the other end to the campground spigot. He always carried an extra length of hose in case the spigot was farther away than one hose would reach.

Hooking up to electricity was as easy as plugging in a toaster. He lifted the heavy black electric cord from its outside storage compartment at the rear of the motorhome and simply inserted the pronged end into the campground outlet. The other end was permanently attached to the motorhome. As he did for the water hose, he also carried on board an extra heavy-duty extension cord for those times when the main cord was too short to reach the campground outlet.

"Now this is the warm weather I expected in Florida!" I said as we stood with Lib watching John begin to unhook the tow car from their motorhome. Paul's and my winter sojourn in Florida happened during an abnormally cold spell. As for our forthcoming trek to Colorado, I could only hope for warm springtime weather.

I hosted at Paul's birthday dinner in the nearby restaurant and at his party in our motorhome immediately after. As the four of us sat at the dinette table in our motorhome, Paul introduced John and Lib to Rummikub®, an intriguing and enjoyable rummy tile game produced by the Pressman Toy Corporation. Our good friends Ava and Ralph Condon had introduced us to the game when we were in Sarasota, Florida, earlier that year.

While Paul explained the rudiments of the game, my eyes took in the scene around me. The four of us sat two on a side at the dinette table on upholstered foam cushions with separate cushioned backs. The fabric is tapestry-like, light blue with white stripes and large white and pinkish-peach flowers. It matches the adjacent, three-cushioned sofa that can be converted into a bed. Across from the sofa is a small computer cabinet with a pullout shelf and a tan plush-upholstered chair held up by a round metal pedestal that allows it to swivel. Above large windows that flank the coach hang oak storage cabinets. All the windows, except those in the driving area, sport Venetian blinds and lined draperies on traverse rods. At night, we draw a beige curtain along a track around the side of the driver's seat and across the front to the middle of the windshield area where we fasten it with Velcro to a similar curtain drawn from the passenger's side.

At the front end of the sofa, the driver's seat faces a dashboard that holds instrumentation for the normal automotive information—fuel gauge, voltage meter, oil pressure gauge, coolant temperature gauge, speedometer, odometer, emergency-brake light, and check light (which warns about a malfunction of the air injection reaction system, which helps to control engine emissions). Our dash also contains a television antenna warning light to let us know when the antenna on the roof is standing upright. This alerts us to lower the antenna before pulling away from a campsite. It helps prevent damage to the antenna when driving under low branches of trees and low roofs on gasoline stations. Paul had added, for his own satisfaction, a transmission-oil temperature gauge, a vacuum gauge (to help us estimate the operation and fuel efficiency of the engine), and a tachometer (to measure the revolutions per minute of the motorhome engine).

Paul had finished explaining how to play Rummikub®, so I turned my attention back to the game. After taking my turn, I glanced forward again. No matter how many other motorhomes I see, I love the layout we have. Across from the driver's seat is a companion passenger's seat; both are electrically operated. Above the windshield, two oak storage cabinets occupy part of the facing that spans from one side of the coach to the other. At the left and right of the facing a round, black speakers for the radio.

Resting on the carpeted hump between the driver and passenger chairs is a 13-inch television set. Its screen faces the rear of the coach and is slightly below eye level to a viewer lounging in the corner of the sofa or sitting in the easy chair. The set is anchored to a small

wooden platform set on a wood pedestal that is inserted into the round opening of a metal plate that is imbedded into the carpeted metal engine cover. Paul would like to move the television so that it hangs above the windshield for more comfortable viewing and more space in the carpeted hump area, but that project has not yet gained first place on his priorities list.

We continued to play our game with its ivory-colored plastic tiles with sets of numbers in different colors. Across the aisle from where we sat stands a stainless steel double sink and beige countertop. Beneath are oak cabinets and a vertical series of drawers for silverware, linens, and utilities such as scissors, pens and clothespins. A four-burner gas stovetop, adjacent to the counter, crowns a pantry with pullout shelves that hold cereals, canned goods, pretzels, and other foodstuffs for the trip. Over the stove is a range hood topped by a microwave/convection oven. Oak cabinets for dishes hang above the sinks and counter.

Alongside the kitchen stands a row of wardrobe closets and cupboards. Across the hallway from them is the bathroom, which contains a shower/tub; a wash basin set in a counter; a toilet on a carpeted platform; wall cabinets; and a framed, lighted mirror above the wash basin. I was pleased that Paul had replaced the original plastic sink with a porcelain one and had also replaced the dual hot and cold faucets with a single mixer faucet on both the sink and the shower.

Paul had made even greater changes in our bedroom at the rear of the motorhome several years earlier. We can now raise the queen-sized bed to reach items stored beneath it. To keep the mattress in place when we're raising the bed and when we make sudden stops while driving, I've placed large sheets of nonslip, rubberized matting between the queen-sized mattress and the wood panel platform on which it rests.

During Paul's bedroom-renovation project, he closed off the rear window that had allowed drafts to flow down on sleepers' heads. On the rear wall he installed matching oak veneer from the Holiday Rambler® factory and a large, four-paneled, beveled mirror that almost covers that wall. Above the mirror is a horizontal row of oak cabinets, just right for bed linens. Above two large windows on either side of the bedroom are wood railings on which we park Paul's baseball caps, small card games, and small books. On each side of the bed in the rear corners is a bedside table with a cabinet beneath. The tabletops serve well for tissues, our travel clocks, and often on mine, scraps of paper or a journal and pen. On the floor in one corner lays a red fire extinguisher. A second red extinguisher hangs beside the entry door steps between the living room swivel chair and kitchen counter.

After four hands of Rummikub®, it was time for refreshments. I retrieved the huge, black leaf bag from the bathroom shower and set it on the bed. Then I removed the cardboard box from the bag. Finally, I lifted the angel food cake from the cardboard box and set it on the bed. The cake was already positioned on a clear acrylic platter. I inserted three candles on the top of the cake, one each for past, present, and future. Shakily in the excitement of the moment, I lit the candles.

When Lib saw me coming toward the dinette table with the cake, she began singing "Happy Birthday." We all joined her—Paul, too. With one mighty puff, Paul blew out the candles. As we ate cake and ice cream, we laughed, kidded one another, and told funny stories. It

"With one mighty puff, Paul blew out the candles."

was a nice birthday, shared with good friends, doing what we loved—traveling by motorhome.

We had left home that morning under overcast skies, then driven through rain all morning and under a cloud cover that afternoon. It was not unusual spring weather, but I hoped for mostly sunshine, especially for driving and sightseeing in future days.

I smiled to myself about how well the arrangements had worked out for Paul's birthday, thanks to Lib and John's gracious participation. Even after driving all day, Paul played Rummikub® and blew out the candles on the cake with gusto.

"It was a nice birthday [Paul's], shared with good friends [Lib and John Graybeal], doing what we loved—traveling by motorhome."

3

Surprise Rendezvous at the Campground

THE RAIN SOUNDED like a host of hummingbirds fluttering their wings on the roof as Paul and I sat at the dinette table in our motorhome eating our breakfast cereal at Spring Valley Campground, Cambridge, Ohio, on Thursday, May 18. Outside our window, a shallow stream pelted by high-splashing raindrops flowed across the gravel road and merged with a pool of rain-mottled, muddy water. I wondered how long the rain and cloudy skies would accompany us. That day was to be a travel day with lunch in Columbus, Ohio, where we planned to meet acquaintances of the Graybeals at a Cracker Barrel Old Country Store®.

Paul said he had thought he might be too wound up to sleep the night before after the first day's travel and his birthday celebration, but he slept easily and soundly until about seven that morning. In addition, our departure time was a leisurely nine o'clock or so. That morning we had only 85 miles to travel to our 11:30 luncheon with Elli and Jack Harper, John and Lib's friends. How relaxing it had been to lie in bed that morning, listening to the rain above me, and not have to get up early.

By 9:20 we were on the road. The windshield wipers squeaked back and forth erasing rain as we followed the Pinnacle and Honda, their red rear lights glowing in the misty morning.

We wore comfortable traveling clothes. Paul had donned a pair of new, wrinkle-free 100 percent cotton trousers. They were light tan and went well with his tan knit shirt with a small design of red and blue blocks. He also wore an avocado green sweater, his everyday one that he liked to have on when he drove. He would probably replace it with his newer light blue one when we went to lunch with the Harpers. I wore a long-sleeved black, green, and white knit pants outfit and my trusty white canvas shoes.

As we rode on I-70 in Ohio, we passed a sign: "Zane Grey Museum." Were it not raining and had I been aware of the museum sooner, I would have asked to stop there. My father, who died when he was 34 and I was 14, had collected and read almost all of the Zane Grey novels. Although I had read only children's books like the Bobbsey Twin series, I had heard him exchanging enthusiastic comments about the Western novels with his friends.

I hoped that we would soon drive out of the rainy front. While I loved to ride along in the cozy motorhome in the rain, I didn't want to get my hair wet. The fine, "permed" strands went limp if I stepped outside in fog or mist or rain. That dampened my motivation to go sightseeing. (Sometimes I wondered how different my life would be if I didn't worry about how my hair looked or—my other worry— how much I weighed!)

My regular hair designer, Marilyn Cross, had done her usual excellent job of cutting and styling my hair on Tuesday, the day before we left on the trip. When we returned, it would be time for my next permanent. Right now, her work was holding up well, and I wanted to do my part to keep it that way. Next Tuesday or Wednesday I would need to ask the Graybeals about stopping at a shopping center for a shampoo and blow-dry.

"Rest area. Wanna stop?" John asked over the CB.

"Yeah, I'll take a break if we have plenty of time," Paul said.

"Okay," John replied.

We turned onto the ramp leading to a rest area, which major interstates provide for travelers. Within five minutes we were back on I-70 West, which was fairly smooth on that stretch—a nice change from the road vibrations of the day before.

Columbus, Ohio, lay 51 miles ahead. We planned to meet the Harpers on the south side of Columbus, north of Wilmington, Ohio.

"Could you turn it down a little more?" I asked Paul as the CB suddenly squawked with static and garbled talk from passing truckers.

"Oh, yeah," said Paul, reaching for the volume dial. Shortly afterward he yawned and switched the windshield wipers to "Intermittent."

At lunch with Elli and Jack Harper, Paul and I got acquainted with these congenial, special friends of John and Lib. Like the Graybeals, they were former campground owners. Jack and John had served together in the late 1970s as board members of the National Campground Owners Association. Jack later served as president of the association and spent considerable time and effort working for the camping industry in Ohio and Washington, D.C. John and Lib try to stop and visit the Harpers at their home near Wilmington, Ohio, whenever they travel in the area. Getting together that day enabled the four of them to get caught up on the news of their mutual friends. The Harpers insisted on treating all of us to lunch. Our interesting and engaging time with them ended too soon, it seemed.

It was after two o'clock when antique enthusiasts John and Lib spotted the I-70 Antique Mall in Springfield, Ohio. We pulled into the mall parking area. Since antique shopping was not something that Paul and I did much of, Paul decided to stay in the motorhome. Ready for a new experience, I traipsed in the misty rain to the huge warehouse. Ever mindful of my hairdo, I protected it with a clear plastic rain cap that tied under my chin.

Lib was already roaming inside. John suggested to me that we all meet in a half-hour at the front door. I looked briefly at my watch.

What a fun place the mall turned out to be! The building interior sported rows and rows of locked cabinets with glass doors and glass shelves, lighted and glowing. I saw inside them dishes, jewelry, toys, dolls—almost anything one could imagine. In another area was a mélange of old objects and furniture. Arranged neatly, all were clean and clearly priced.

A Structo metal toy fire engine (which was accompanied by the original, though now ragged, packaging box) attracted me. Grandmother Beard gave our son, Jeff, one like it for Christmas many years ago. We still had it in our basement. The asking price was $200! That old fire engine is apparently one item that my heirs will be glad I saved when they are cleaning out our household "junk."

The half-hour vanished quickly. I told Lib as we left the mall that I enjoyed making unexpected stops rather than going pell-mell to a destination. She said, "Well, we *are* on vacation!" This was a favorite expression of hers when anyone suggested that we ought to get up early in the morning or hurry somewhere.

"Now this is the kind of trip I like," I told Paul as I returned to our motorhome, unable to contain my excitement.

"I'm glad that you're enjoying yourself," he smiled in his good-natured way.

By four o'clock, we passed a sign just across the Indiana state line that said "The People of Indiana Welcome You." A half-hour later, we paused at a rest stop near mile marker 144 in Indiana. In hard rain, John came over with his *Trailer Life Directory for Campgrounds, RV Parks & Services*. We liked his suggestion of going to Cloverdale RV Park beyond Indianapolis to camp that night.

Rain, rain, and more rain fell as we headed toward Indianapolis. The radio reported that racers preparing for the Indy 500 could practice on the track only one hour that day because of the rain. The sky ahead looked very dark and threatening. Over the CB, when John asked Paul what he thought we should do, Paul said we should keep going and see what we could find. I would have been tempted to pull over at the next safe parking area.

All along I-70 we saw water standing in fields. Many areas had been recently plowed, others newly planted with corn. One farmer being interviewed on the radio said he was more fortunate than many others because he had already planted his corn. He would wait until the rainwater disappeared to see how much he needed to reseed. The spring had apparently been quite rainy, which meant that many farmers had to delay planting until the fields dried enough.

I looked over anxiously at Paul when I heard the radio announcer warn of flood watches and tornadoes. Muddy water gushed along in roadside ditches and in swollen streams.

On we went, splashing down I-70 and into downtown Indianapolis during rush-hour traffic. At one point, we crept in a long line of vehicles with the rain pouring down on us all.

West of Indianapolis, we turned off I-70 at exit 41 and drove about a mile to Cloverdale RV Park. We pulled up in front of the campground office to register. I saw what looked like a body of water through leafy trees behind the office building. I wondered if the possibility of flooding would threaten my peace of mind during the night.

From habit, I retrieved from the glove compartment our membership benefit cards for Paul to take along into the office. Paul registered for us. I sat up tall in the passenger seat trying to discern what that body of water was. Then I used a small calculator from the glove compartment to figure our mileage for the day. We had driven 323 miles that second day on the road, slightly less than the 344 of the first day.

Soon Paul opened the driver's side door of the motorhome and got behind the wheel. He said, "We won't have to worry about flooding here tonight. The reason they were so full is because they are the only campground in the area not under water. That water you saw back of those trees is only a reservoir-type pond."

With his tone being so positive, I let go of my concern.

At our campsite, Paul hooked up the motorhome to water and electricity. Even in wet conditions, he much prefers doing that to carrying suitcases into a motel or hotel. We ate supper and watched the news on television. A flood watch was in effect for Morgan County, which was where we were. It continued to rain off and on, although the weather forecaster said that the rain would not be in the form of thunderstorms.

After watching the news, between rain showers, Paul walked up to the campground office and store to look around. John had told Paul that Lib was settled in for the night, so I decided to put on my pajamas and robe and relax as I watched television. I had just finished changing clothes when Paul opened the door and said, "Guess who's parked in front of us?"

It was his second cousin, Jesse Yingling; his wife, Emagene; and their granddaughter, Christine Martens. They were en route in their travel trailer from their full-time campsite near Edinburgh, Texas, to Ohio, their former home, to attend a wedding and to take care of some other matters. Paul and I had visited them in Texas on an earlier trip

". . . Paul opened the door and said, 'Guess who's parked in front of us?' It was his second cousin, Jesse Yingling; his wife, Emagene; and their granddaughter, Christine Martens."

from Maryland to Arizona in our motorhome. They subsequently visited us at our home in Maryland.

Paul told me that as he walked on a narrow path to the office, ahead of him was Jesse and ahead of Jesse was Emagene. He saw only their backs and didn't recognize them—they were intent on getting to the laundry. As Paul browsed in the store, Jesse came in from the laundry, whereupon they recognized one another. How exciting!

"I told them to come over."

"But I'm like this," I said, gesturing to my lounging outfit.

"That's okay. Nothing wrong with that," he said. "I'm going over to talk with John and Lib at their motorhome about what time we'll leave tomorrow morning."

I changed back to day clothes again. Paul returned from the Graybeals' and shortly afterward Jesse knocked on our motorhome door. Emagene and Christine were finishing up at the laundry, but they soon arrived too. Having been tour guides of the western states for Old Order Amish tourists, Jesse and Emagene gave us enthusiastic suggestions on what to see along our way and in Colorado. It was after 11:00 when we hugged those heartwarming family members good-bye. Meeting them added serendipity and enjoyment to our second day on the road.

The next day would be a fuller day of travel as we headed toward the Harry S. Truman Library in Independence, Missouri. Never having visited a presidential library and museum, I was curious about what it would offer. A tour book had said the Truman museum had a replica of the Oval Office in the White House, the very table used for signing the United Nations charter, and the graves of President and Mrs. Truman.

As for the rain and clouds, I could only hope they would give way to sunshine the next day.

4

Harry S. Truman
Library and Museum

I WAS UP, eating a leisurely breakfast, enjoying the sunny morning at Cloverdale RV Park in Indiana, and looking forward to getting back on the road. We didn't know how far we would go that Friday, but we would head toward Independence, Missouri, and its Harry S. Truman Library. That meant passing through Illinois and most of Missouri, almost to Kansas.

From the corner of my eye, I noticed John outside his motorhome.

"It looks like John is unhooking their electricity. What time were we supposed to leave?" I asked Paul, who had been up just long enough to get dressed.

"Maybe we've driven into a different time zone," Paul said as he stepped down into the motorhome stairwell and unlocked the entry door.

I thought I'd gotten up two hours ahead of our departure time, my usual practice. That allowed plenty of time to wash up, brush my teeth, put on makeup, dress, eat breakfast, pray, and read a chapter in the Bible. It started my day off well.

After talking with John, Paul returned and said that they indeed were ready to leave, that the campground was on eastern *standard* time, which was one hour earlier than eastern *daylight* time. Paul's and my clocks and watches were still set on eastern daylight time. Paul hurriedly ate his breakfast and went outside to unhook our water and electricity from the campground post.

Meanwhile, I prepared the inside of our motorhome to leave the campsite—wound down the television antenna; turned off the furnace, water heater, and water pump; and made sure anything out on counters was put away and that the refrigerator/freezer doors were locked. My eyes had become accustomed to sweeping the inside perimeter of the coach before departure. As I saw what should be put away, I stowed it so that it would not fall to the floor as we traveled down the highway.

In the end, we left only about 20 minutes later than our planned 8:30 A.M. departure time from Cloverdale RV Park in west-central Indiana.

Continuing west on I-70 in Indiana, we headed toward Independence, Missouri. I felt a little tired that morning compared with how peaceful and rested I had felt the morning before. Small wonder—yesterday's rain had given me anxious moments; also, I had gone to bed later than my usual time. Since I was tired, I thought Paul must be even more so because he had driven all day. So I asked him, "Would you like me to take a turn at driving?"

He knew I could drive the motorhome; he was the one who had encouraged and taught me. Before we bought our motorhome, he had said that he would not want to get one if I didn't drive it also. Always ready to say yes and take on a challenge, I agreed. But that was before the monstrous vehicle was a reality. Once we brought home our brand new, Moby Dick of a motorhome, I delayed learning to drive it. It intimidated me. My fears included images of driving too close to the inside wall of a tunnel and causing an accident involving other motorists. I knew I had to conquer my negative thoughts, but it was difficult to even get into the driver's seat. I put it off until Paul suggested a dry run in our driveway. That seemed safe enough.

During that driveway session, Paul gently gave me suggestions. By the end, I had become familiar with turning on and off the ignition, moving the gearshift lever and windshield wipers, looking at the side view mirrors, setting and using the cruise control, checking the various dials on the dash, and pushing switches that electrically moved the driver's seat to accommodate my requirements. I learned that the motorhome was a foot and a half wider than our Lincoln two-door car, and I got a sense of where to position the motorhome on the road. Later I learned that looking ahead four or five car lengths and focusing on the middle of my lane of traffic would easily place the motorhome between the lines of my lane.

Paul told me that because of the heavy weight of the motorhome, I should begin to slow down sooner than I would in a car. Also, when I turned a corner, I should allow room for the rear end of the motorhome to swing in the opposite direction of the turn.

That was my initial lesson. A few days later, Paul drove the motorhome to an interstate dual-lane highway and pulled over onto the wide shoulder. We switched seats and I had my initiation into driving our new motorhome on the road. After about six miles, I left the highway and drove about 17 more miles on a two-lane road, part of which went through a small town with cars parked on each side of its main street. I then practiced on dirt country roads, with Paul always encouraging me and giving suggestions.

Each time I got behind the wheel, I had to overcome my fears. I had seen women driving big yellow school buses, and that gave me inspiration and motivation. But it wasn't until I had more experience on an actual trip that I put aside my negative thoughts and gained confidence.

When we started out on one of our first trips—a three-week trip from Maryland to Oregon—Paul had bursitis in his right shoulder joint. That put me in the driver's seat. By the end of the second day, I was driving on the freeway on the south side of Chicago at evening rush hour, keeping up with traffic—including trucks on both sides—going the maximum speed allowed.

On that trip, I encountered most of my imagined difficult circumstances—road construction, concrete walls, tunnels, bridges, and traffic—and the motorhome and vehicles I shared the road with came through without a scratch. The more I drove, the less intimidated I became. I found that once I got behind the wheel, a feeling of exhilaration and power came over me and I sallied forth fearlessly, keeping in mind the various instructions and rules Paul had given me. I liked the way that people waved to me from the street when they saw a woman at the wheel. I was ready to drive on the Colorado trip if Paul needed a rest.

"No. I'd just as soon drive. I wouldn't sleep anyway like you do in the passenger seat," Paul said. Paul has always been a light sleeper, finding it hard to get to sleep and being easily awakened.

One great aspect about that Friday was the *sunshine*. For two days we had driven in rain. How pleasant it was to ride under a cloudless blue sky with only the faint, white, three-quarter moon floating ahead of us.

I-70 cut through Indiana with its dual lanes at times separated by patches of trees. On the shoulder of the interstate, a wee black bird paused, pigeon-toed, on spindly legs as we approached, cocked its head sidewise, then quickly flew out of sight.

As we passed mile marker 126, water stood in small pools in the fields on either side of the highway, but the scene was nothing like we had encountered the day before.

About nine o'clock we crossed the Illinois state line and read a roadside sign: "The People of Illinois Welcome You."

When we stopped at a rest area at mile marker 147, a huge tractor-trailer pulled in beside John and Lib. John said he thought a woman was driving it. Paul, John, and I stood at the rear of the enormous vehicle watching as the driver maneuvered it precisely where it should be between the parking lines, even backing it up to make it just right. We waited to see the driver. To our surprise, a young woman climbed down from the driver's seat.

A short time later, as Paul and I pulled away from that rest area, Paul opened his window to speak to the tractor-trailer driver. By that time, she was controlling two small black dogs by their leashes in the grassy pet area beside the driveway.

"Ma'am," Paul said, "would you tell me how long that trailer is?"

"Fifty-three feet, and the whole length is 72 feet," she said congenially. She added that a 400 CAT engine powered the tractor part of the rig.

We moved on, soon regaining I-70.

"The water in the Wabash River is up a little, if you look to your right," Paul said.

I began to record in my spiral tablet the flooding I saw on either side of I-70.

10:27 A.M.   Little Wabash River surges under I-70. Fields flooded, merging with the river's muddy water.

10:59 A.M.   Kaskaskia River, IL. Huge area of water just prior to Kaskaskia. Muddy.

11:28 P.M.   Shoal River. Way up; muddy, almost touches underpart of bridge; fields flooded nearby.

12:59 P.M.   Missouri River. Muddy, swollen, wide expanse of water, floating logs, etc.

1:00 P.M.   Missouri state line. Crossing bridge over Missouri River.

1:04 P.M.   Two-mile backup of traffic on eastbound lane toward Missouri River bridge where crew worked at something over the side of the bridge, per John.

1:21 P.M.   Missouri River (again). Casino parking lot was under water. Also road toward it looks under about three feet of muddy, brown water.

3:41 P.M.	Missouri River (again). Expansive flooding nearby; great fields of muddy water.
4:03 P.M.	Chouteau Creek. Way over its banks onto fields. Muddy water seeming to stand there.
4:06 P.M.	"Lamine River's up too," Paul said. It overflows into woods, around trees, and into fields.
4:23 P.M.	Blackwater River. Overflowing. Large fields under water.

"My word, what's coming up?" I asked, looking ahead at water everywhere on both sides of the highway. It was 4:36 P.M.

"Looks like it's already up," said Paul, referring to Davis Creek. The swollen creek paid no attention to its normal boundaries. A frontage road that led to a house lay under water, leaving the house stranded. Flooded fields looked like large brown lakes.

The people of that area must have been grateful for a day without rain. Seeing the flooded region sobered me. Along the way, we had seen flood waters surround mobile homes. At one place only half a mailbox showed above the water. I had never lived close to a flood basin. Now the hardships associated with too much rain were real to me. People here had to cope. They had lost precious treasures, mementos, and financial assets. They needed faith, courage, patience, and determination.

When television newscasters reported floods in the future, I would relate realistically with the scenes and people. I was learning experientially that the best way to understand someone or some event was to talk with that person or visit that scene. The truck driver turned out to be a charming person; the flood scenes that day opened my eyes to the actual damage that floods do.

After a long travel day, 446 miles, we arrived at Trailside Campers Inn of Kansas City, Grain Valley, Missouri, at 5:46 P.M. We were just a few miles outside Independence, our goal for that day.

As usual we registered, found our sites, which were side by side, and hooked up to utilities. The Graybeals and we ate dinner in our individual coaches. Afterward, John unhooked the tow car so that he and Lib could go to the local grocery store. Paul and I joined them. I had run out of bananas. We also needed more paper cups, individual-serving cans of fruit, and snack-type pudding cups. Paul browsed the bakery department and selected a jumbo blueberry muffin for us to share as a snack that evening. The Graybeals needed peanuts and ice cream, two of John's daily favorites.

We returned to the campground, thanked and said good night to our friends, and stepped up into our familiar home. After putting away the groceries, I totaled the expenses and mileage for the day in my trip log. Meanwhile, Paul retrieved the glass cleaner from under the kitchen sink, reached for the blue plastic footstool that we keep in the living room area behind the passenger seat, and went outside to clean the bugs off the windshield. He checked the oil levels in the engine and auxiliary generator as he often did to prepare for the next day's travel. After our easy tasks we enjoyed watching television. Paul ate his half of the muffin, with lots of milk, before going to bed. I planned to eat my half of the muffin as dessert at lunchtime the next day.

The next morning, in bright sunshine, we climbed into the Graybeals' tow car and found our way to the Harry S. Truman Library, on the northeast edge of U.S. 24 at Delaware Street, Independence, Missouri. We arrived five minutes ahead of the 9 A.M. opening time. Only a few other people walked the peaceful grounds in the fresh, early morning air. We paused in front of a replica of the Liberty Bell on the spacious, tree-shaded lawn. I snapped a picture of two "ding dongs," as Lib laughingly described John and Paul, while they pretended to lift the heavy bell with one hand. Soon we strolled toward the modern, columned library and museum, situated atop a small knoll.

We were among the first visitors to the library on that Saturday morning. Just inside the impressive marble foyer stood a genial man in uniform. He told me that admission was free to the library and museum while the building underwent renovations that included asbestos removal. While we were unable to see the Oval Office replica area, we saw a film about President Truman; the east wing, which contained a museum; and the Trumans' graves. The renovation

"We paused in front of a replica of the Liberty Bell on the spacious, tree-shaded lawn. I snapped a picture of two 'ding dongs,' as Lib laughingly described John and Paul, while they pretended to lift the heavy bell with one hand." (L-R: Paul and John)

project was a major part of celebrating the 50th anniversary of the beginning of the Truman presidency (1945–1953).

The table on which the United Nations charter was signed, normally on exhibit at the Truman library, had been sent to San Francisco for the 50-year anniversary of the charter signing. The greeter said the table had a blue felt cover. Underneath, much to his disappointment, the tabletop was simply plywood; it came apart in three sections. He thought it would be mahogany or some other fine wood, but not so. The table was about nine feet in diameter and round, not oval as I had imagined. It was essentially a stage prop, intended to be used only for the ceremonial signing of the United Nations charter.

A short film, *An Ordinary Man in Extraordinary Times*—an apt label for President Truman—told of Truman's farm background and his simple life. We walked through the museum with its exhibits of gifts and portraits. I saw the folding chair on which Truman sat at the Democratic convention when he was nominated vice president.

Inside the museum, near the courtyard, a friendly staff member stood behind a high counter. He answered my questions and told me

"Soon we strolled toward the modern, columned [Truman] library and museum, situated atop a small knoll. We were among the first visitors to the library on that Saturday morning." [L-R: Paul, Lib, and John]

that he had known Truman personally. The staff member had formerly delivered bread to the Kroger and A&P stores in Independence. When he delivered to the Kroger store, he would see Truman taking his morning walk and occasionally talked with him. At the A&P store, he delivered Upside Down Bread to Bess Truman every day. Sometimes he handed it to her personally. Otherwise, he put a note on it saying it was for Mrs. Truman.

When Mrs. Truman provided for the donation of the family home to the U.S. government in her will, she reserved the use of the second floor for Margaret Truman Daniels, the Trumans' daughter, for her lifetime.

The film and the president's ground-level tombstone in the courtyard called Truman a "judge." The four of us (John, Lib, Paul, and I) puzzled over that nomenclature—we had not heard of any law education in Truman's background. The staff member told me that Judge was an administrative position at the time and that Truman had no law degree and in fact never earned a college degree.

The Harry S. Truman Library is operated by the National Archives and Records Administration. The research room is open to the public; the staff will make President Truman's papers available to anyone. The library has a web site (www.trumanlibrary.org) on which all of its documents are described and a few thousand of them are available on line for reading and printing out. Some people work many years on their research projects. The library's 15 million pages of papers are in locked stack areas. The library staff continues to work at making some of these documents available on line. The library also contains extensive collections of photographs, motion picture films, and audio recordings. The manuscripts, photographs, films, and audio recordings, along with the more than 30,000 museum objects, bring researchers from all over the world to the library.

Even though our visit was curtailed by renovations, I was glad for the opportunity to gain more knowledge and a much better appreciation of President Truman than I had when I entered the museum. I remembered that when he was in office, many people, including myself, thought of him as almost a nonentity in the White House. He played the piano and sang "Happy Birthday." He fired General MacArthur. He had a sign on his desk: "The buck stops here." But after touring the museum, I had a true respect for President Truman, although I'm not a member of his political party. I found that the Trumans were down-to-earth people. I saw that Truman's integrity stemmed from his Midwestern, hardworking upbringing. He never sought praise for himself, he just did the best job he could—which was commendable in my opinion. His values served both him and us well.

Our visit to the Harry S. Truman Library had been so heart-warming. I wondered how it would compare with the Eisenhower Center, which we hoped to visit the next day when we reached Kansas.

5

Eisenhower Center

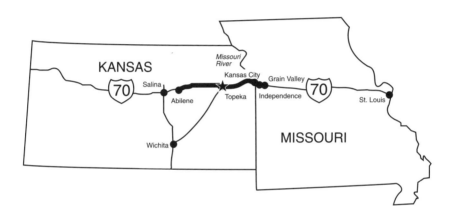

THE HARRY S. TRUMAN Library in Independence, Missouri, was the main topic of our conversation on that sunny Saturday morning as we rode away in the Honda. Back at our campsites at Trailside Campers Inn of Kansas City in Grain Valley, Missouri, John hitched the tow car to their motorhome while Paul unhooked our coach from its utilities and I prepared the interior for travel on the road. At 11:05 A.M., still under sunny skies, our two-RV caravan pulled out of the campground, heading toward Abilene, Kansas, only 185 miles west on I-70. Our main objective in Abilene was, of course, to tour the Eisenhower Center the following day. I particularly wanted to visit the chapel on the grounds, since it would be Sunday morning when I would ordinarily be in church if I were at home. I didn't know, of course, if my agenda would work out with the others.

At the Kansas Welcome Center and Motor Vehicle Inspection Station, off of I-70, we ate lunch in our coaches while parked in the paved area for RVs. Afterward, John, Paul, and I visited the welcome center itself, culling literature about Abilene and Kansas.

One of the activities I enjoy when traveling is sending post-cards—ones that always seem to jump out at me as being so right for certain friends that I just must send them. I couldn't resist buying a card that showed huge, yellow Kansas sunflowers. It was perfect for Joyce Dell, a member of our local camping group who had bought an outfit with a sunflower design during one of our outings; who had been presented with a hat with a sunflower design at her recent retirement from a laudable, client-devoted career in social services; and who is an artist and craftsperson who loves tole painting and the happy colors of sunflowers. She paints them on earrings and pins and decorates wood items such as plaques that are skillfully made by her husband, Carroll, in his woodworking shop.

After lunch, as we continued on I-70 toward Topeka, Kansas, a few raindrops hit our windshield. At least we'd had sunshine for our visit to the Truman museum that morning.

We were enjoying the smooth highway when John and Paul began discussing a problem that had just begun with the CB and cruise control in John's RV. The cruise control momentarily lost its speed control when John talked into the CB. Paul and he puzzled over it, with Paul asking questions. They could only conclude that per-haps the chassis battery was too low to furnish power to both the cruise control and CB, which were hooked to the same power supply. Also, they speculated, perhaps the battery needed water.

After traveling 185 miles from Grain Valley, Missouri, we regis-tered at the Covered Wagon RV Park, Abilene, Kansas, about 3:30 P.M. in rainy weather. After connecting our motorhomes to water and electricity, we set out in the tow car to see Abilene and have dinner somewhere that offered steaks. John said he thought that good steaks should be available in Kansas. The brochures that we had picked up earlier at the Kansas welcome center suggested Abilene attractions we could visit before dinner.

As we drove around town, we spotted the Museum of Independent Telephony at 412 South Campbell Street. Our brochure informed us that it was open until 8 P.M. Since Paul was a retired telephone man, that museum was a natural attraction for us.

Inside, we paid the small admission fee and picked up a leaflet that provided information for a self-guided tour. The museum was a large room that contained an excellent collection of well-organized objects with easily readable signs to identify them. I saw and gently touched a replica of Alexander Graham Bell's first telephone. I saw the old-time magneto telephone wall sets with the ringer on the side, similar to one I had used on the farm where I grew up.

A sliced section of telephone cable showed the wires inside surrounded by a lead sleeve. When Paul was first with the telephone company, he worked as a cable splicer's helper, and he had talked to me many times about lead sleeves. As we traveled on various roads in our car, he would point out an enlarged place in the telephone cable overhead that he had helped to repair. I had never seen what was inside them until I visited this museum.

Paul had told me that when there was trouble in a telephone line, the cable splicer would climb the pole, slit lengthwise the lead sleeve of the cable where the trouble was thought to be, repair the wires inside, and then cover the section with a new piece of lead sleeve.

As the helper, Paul would select the correct diameter of lead sleeve from their supplies, cut off a piece the proper length (the length of the exposed section of the cable plus a few inches of overlap on each end), slit it lengthwise, and send the new sleeve up to the splicer by a rope-and-pulley system.

Paul then heated solder in a lead pot to just the right temperature. Using a pulley system, he raised the lead pot to the work area of the splicer, who soldered shut the lengthwise slit. After tapping down the ends of the new lead sleeve so that they clasped the cable, the splicer then soldered the ends to be sure the repair was airtight. One time the splicer accidentally tipped the lead pot of hot solder.

Had Paul not been watching closely, the hot lead would have come down on him. He and the splicer did their work in conditions ranging from snowy and windy weather to hot summer temperatures.

Later, Paul was transferred to the inside equipment area, where he enjoyed learning about electronics and circuitry and went to every telephone training class offered. By the time he retired, he was a long-distance technician. People in other offices and departments of the company often called him when they had a problem that stymied them. He had consistently made a practice of learning the equipment and understanding its operating principles.

The museum contained more styles and colors of round glass telephone insulators than I knew existed—86 different hues. Insulators were screwed onto threaded wooden pins inserted into holes in the wooden crossarms affixed to telephone poles. The telephone line was wired in ("tied into" in telephone lingo) the circular groove of the glass insulator. This arrangement kept the current traveling along the telephone line in order to complete its circuit from one location to another. If the current went down the pole to the ground instead, the circuit would be shorted and fail, and people would lose their telephone service.

The museum also housed replicas of a telephone office, of actual telephone booths, and of switchboards that gave visitors an opportunity to play operator.

Paul and I walked along looking at and commenting about various objects. I wondered if the Graybeals were enjoying the museum since they did not have the same telephone company interests that we did. Fresh out of high school, Lib had worked as a secretary with the local gas and electric company as I had. She stopped working to rear her family of four children. After her husband died suddenly of a heart attack, she became a teacher's assistant in a nearby public school. When she married John, one daughter was married, the other two lived on their own, and the youngest, a son, was still in school and lived at home. With a natural sense of style and love of fashion, Lib has ably served as a volunteer model for area fashion shows. She belongs to the Federation of Woman's Clubs and likes to play golf.

John had lost his wife suddenly from a cerebral hemorrhage. He had three boys—two were on their own at the time of their mother's death and one was in college. John's career was in public education; he had served as a teacher, high school principal, and director of personnel. He also had established a campground, planning and building it from scratch. Lib and John both enjoy motorhoming and their two families united in harmony, just as the two of them did. John laughingly remarked that one of his requirements for a second wife was that she like to travel, but I have a hunch that he would have married Lib anyway, even if she hadn't been willing to travel by RV. John is also an avid golfer. For 15 years after his early retirement, he was a volunteer income tax preparer for senior citizens, among other volunteer positions. Both he and Lib belong to and are active in the local historical society.

In the museum, I noticed that John and Lib sauntered along just as we did. The four of us talked back and forth about our discoveries. I was learning that our speeds of looking at items in museums were compatible.

From the telephone museum, John drove us to the Kirby House at 205 N.E. Third Street for dinner. The Italianate-style Victorian two-story house was built in 1885 by banker Thomas Kirby and subsequently turned into apartments. It had been restored into a first-class, fine dining restaurant. The mâitre d' gave us the choice of dining downstairs or upstairs. We chose the latter. Upstairs, four carpeted dining rooms were decorated with filigreed wallpaper, stenciled ceilings, and mauve and white tablecloths.

John wanted a good Kansas steak, so he ordered beef, as did Lib and Paul. I ordered a pork tenderloin. The food was delicious. We relaxed and talked about the telephone museum, the Kirby House's interior decorations, and the fact that the servers had to carry food from the kitchen to the second floor. We wondered if they used the front entry stairs as we had.

Lib, Paul, and I declined dessert, but John tried the brown cinnamon ice cream, which Lib and I tasted. We declared it "pretty good."

As we left the table, I asked the server if the restaurant had a dumbwaiter on the second floor and if I might see it. Such equipment having to do with food interests me. We had a dumbwaiter on the farm. When it was resting on the level of our country kitchen, it was housed behind wooden cabinet doors. We would open them to place on it what we wanted to keep cold, such as butter, jelly, bread, and opened glass jars of peaches. By hand, we would lower the wooden shelves suspended by ropes into the basement, where the temperature was always cool, and close the doors on the kitchen level. Then we'd bring up the dumbwaiter when we had a meal. It moved up and down easily.

But my interest in food service really began in the years when my mother ran a restaurant and catering service. After my father's death, the tombstone salesman came to the farm. A kind man, he wanted to help my mother by trying to find her a job. He knew we would have to move off the farm and in with my grandparents. When he asked if she wanted to work in the sewing factory, she said, "No sewing for this chicken. Cookin's my line!" He subsequently got her a job as a cook at the Charles Carroll Hotel, the only hotel in Westminster, Maryland.

After working there seven days a week for several years, during which time my grandfather died and our family of two widows and four daughters moved into Westminster, she opened her own eating establishment and catering service in our home in town. She named it Sunset View Inn and served meals by reservation only for groups in the community—mainly families and clubs for dinners—and catered receptions and other special occasions.

After attending high school classes during the day, I served as a waitress at the hotel when my mother was a cook there. After graduation and with a full-time job as a secretary at the local gas and electric company, I often helped my mother as a waitress. It seemed only natural that when I went to other eating places I would be interested in what went on behind the scenes.

Once I had asked to see the kitchen of a restaurant at the Waldorf-Astoria in New York, where I was staying in order to attend a conference connected with my work as an assistant director of college admissions. A nice gentleman gave me a grand tour. I felt close to the people who worked there, just as I had at my mother's home.

I discovered that the Kirby House, with eating rooms on both levels, had developed an intriguing arrangement for food service. Our server enthusiastically ushered me to rooms at the rear of the house on the second floor. She pointed to the far side of one of the rooms, where I saw a stainless steel, three-shelved opening about three feet by four feet. She told me that they mainly used the dumbwaiter for sending dirty dishes downstairs and that they usually carried the meals upstairs on trays.

A back stairway that I saw as I left the dumbwaiter room apparently was the one they used for carrying the food upstairs. Otherwise, they would be carrying trays of food in the main hallway and up the stairs where customers came and went.

I hurried to rejoin the others in the downstairs hallway. On that rainy, misty evening, we returned to the campground and agreed to start for the Eisenhower Center about 9:00 A.M. the next day.

Then, cozy in our motorhome, Paul joined me in watching an episode of *Dr. Quinn—Medicine Woman*. At dinner that night, Lib had mentioned wanting to get back to the coach in time to see the show. It was Dr. Quinn's wedding day.

Sunday morning, May 21, arrived rainy and cool. About 8:45 John drove us in the tow car to the Eisenhower Center, S.E. 4th Street in Abilene. A complex of buildings and grounds situated on a level plain, it seemed a fitting memorial because it looked both noble and peaceful. Although former President Eisenhower was a general who had led the United States to a successful conclusion of World War II, he actually advocated peace and adherence to democratic principles.

The center included the Dwight D. Eisenhower Library, a visitor center, the family home, a museum, and the Place of Meditation. An 11-foot, bronze, military statue of Eisenhower on a five-sided pedestal of Georgia granite stood toward one end of the enormous lawn. A generous parking area was provided adjacent to the visitor center and family home. This time, I hoped to see a reproduction of the Oval Office.

We arrived at the visitor center just in time to see the first showing of the Eisenhower film. The next showing would have been at 10 A.M. Only one other couple sat in the large auditorium with us and watched a depicting of the life and work of Dwight D. Eisenhower.

After viewing the film, we visited the adjoining gift shop. We bought two souvenir cups for Nancy and Jeff with the names of the presidents on them and stored them immediately in the car. From there, we strolled over to the Eisenhower family home. Situated on its original location, it was the two-story, wood-frame home where Ike and his brothers grew up. The Eisenhowers lived there from 1898 until 1946. When Ike's mother, Mrs. Ida Elizabeth Stover Eisenhower, died in 1946, her sons gave the structure, family furniture, and mementos as they were at the time of their mother's death to the Eisenhower Foundation.

A friendly man serving as a tour guide greeted us in the front hallway. He showed us through the three small front rooms down-

"From there, we strolled over to the Eisenhower family home. Situated on its original location, it was the two-story, wood-frame home where Ike and his brothers grew up." (L-R: the author and Lib)

stairs. The upstairs was not open to visitors. Toward the rear of the house, a woman guide told us that the dining room in which we stood was formerly the kitchen. She pointed to a credenza where a large cookstove used to sit. The credenza itself was a secondhand piece that Ike's mother bought for $5. A small kitchen had been added to the back of the house. Also, the guide told us the house was on the "wrong" or "poor" side of the railroad tracks that ran near it. Altogether, the house looked small for a family with six boys (one son had died young).

The museum ($2.50 per person for those over 62) offered a surprise—in addition to oil paintings by Eisenhower and Winston Churchill, it displayed watercolors by, of all people, Adolf Hitler! I was amazed by Hitler's innocent-looking watercolors. Churchill's paintings had a strong, bold feel. Eisenhower's early work seemed primitive, but his skill grew, as apparent in his later paintings.

I was also surprised to see Eisenhower's staff car among the extensive exhibits. A Cadillac, it was painted a dull khaki and had over 200,000 miles on the odometer. We spent almost two hours wandering among the engaging maze of presidential gifts and artifacts. It was well worth our time and interest. The one disappointment of the Eisenhower Center was that it did not have a reproduction of the Oval Office. Perhaps someday I would get to see the real one, I mused.

The museum building was constructed of Kansas limestone. It was built by the Eisenhower Foundation, whose funds came from gifts from the public.

From the museum we strolled on a long pavement leading to the Place of Meditation. A modest, A-frame structure with a steeple tower in front, the chapel was also built of native limestone and blended with the modern architecture of the library and museum.

On that Sunday morning, I especially wanted to have some prayer time, so I stepped into the building. Just inside, Dwight D. Eisenhower, Mamie Doud Eisenhower, and their firstborn son, Doud Dwight, were buried. I stood for a few moments of veneration looking down at the flat, ground-level, engraved stones at their grave sites. I listened to the trickling water moving down the wall at the head of the graves.

Then I walked to my right around that wall into a small sanctuary. My travel mates entered and sat there, too, quietly. I looked at the multicolored windowpanes, then closed my eyes in prayer. I let my thoughts reach out to God. In that brief time I relaxed. I knew I would always remember those sacred moments in that special place for meditation.

The Dwight D. Eisenhower Library was open for research only on Monday through Friday, so we were unable to see that facility on a Sunday morning. From a brochure, I learned that its exterior was Kansas limestone. Inside, it must have been magnificent with its extensive use of imported marble. It too was built with contributions from gifts of friends and admirers of President Eisenhower. The library is administered by the National Archives and Records Administration, just as the Truman library is.

These two Midwestern men, Truman and Eisenhower, one Democrat and the other Republican, led our country well as presidents. Neither put on a great show or seemed to seek acclamation. Both came from poor families, yet they each worked hard and dutifully, and their work led eventually into the White House. Their work ethic served them well.

As we left the peaceful Eisenhower Center that Sunday morning and headed for the campground to retrieve our motorhomes and push on toward Dodge City, I chuckled when I thought about the contrast between the place we had just left and our next sightseeing stop, known as the "Wickedest Little City in America." I wondered just how wicked Dodge City would be.

6

Wickedest Little City in America

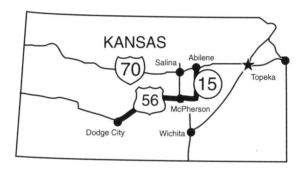

AFTER OUR TOUR of the peaceful Eisenhower Center in Abilene, Kansas, on Sunday morning, Lib, John, Paul, and I returned to the Covered Wagon RV Park. We ate lunch early in our motorhomes and unhooked from the utilities. Then, a few minutes after noon, we drove away in dripping rain. Dodge City was 222 miles west. We wanted to bunk down there that evening and tour that famous Wild West cattle town of the late 1800s the next day.

On the map, Route 15 from Abilene, Kansas, south to U.S. 56 looked like a spindly country road, one not suitable for two long motorhomes. John, however, had talked with a man at the Abilene campground where we had stayed who told him it would be a nice drive.

We proceeded amid great meadows with grazing beef cattle and comfortable farm homes, barns, and huge silos nestled here and there on the horizon. The rain had stopped; clouds overhung the scene. The smooth asphalt road led straight ahead and was raised above the adjacent land.

I was using the laptop computer again that day. I was rather amazed that I had been typing into the computer each day, at last getting into the habit of using that particular device. It was fun to be creative while looking at the countryside. I could write much more compared to writing by hand in a tablet and look out at the countryside simultaneously.

Paul drove with one hand on the steering wheel and the other resting on his right thigh. He wore his royal blue National Bank of Alaska cap; a long-sleeved, white knit shirt; gray shantung trousers; and his familiar avocado green sweater.

I wore a two-piece royal blue sweat suit, sleeves pushed up, and silver earrings. Navy anklets and white canvas loafers completed my outfit.

As usual, Paul and John had the CBs on to communicate as the need arose. That day the cruise control and CB worked well on the Graybeals' motorhome.

The only other equipment problem on the trip came that morning when Paul was shaving and our water pump did not operate. After he looked at the water pump, located in the bedside cabinet at the rear of the motorhome, and asked me to operate the pump switch above the entry door a few times, the problem seemed to be resolved. So all was okay at the moment. One never knew, of course, when another problem would surface, but that was part of RV traveling.

We passed enormous, graceful fields of grain, with some areas of swirling green stalks beaten down by rain or hail.

As our two motorhomes neared McPherson, Kansas, a city of 15,000, we hoped to see one of our Church of the Brethren colleges. None of us had visited it before or knew its address. Founded in 1887, McPherson College was an independent, residential, liberal arts college that welcomed students of all faiths.

Suddenly we saw a brick building on our right with huge letters spelling "McPherson College." John soon turned right on nearby Eby Street. Paul and I followed, wending our way through a maze of streets, hoping to find a parking lot large enough for our vehicles.

As we maneuvered closer to the college itself, my excitement leaped even higher when John said over the CB that he and Lib saw people in caps and gowns. We found a large parking lot on the McPherson College campus.

After taking a picture of the McPherson Church of the Brethren on campus and touring the adjacent church school building, I hurried to the center plaza to see if it was really commencement day and, if so, to watch the outdoor processional.

Students and faculty wearing academic regalia scurried up the steps into Miller Library. The scene seemed heartwarmingly familiar to me. As a former coordinator for commencement ceremonies at Western Maryland College in my job as executive assistant, I felt excited to be back at a college again at such an important time in these students' lives.

The husband of a graduate waited on the sidewalk. He said the processional would come from the library across the street, make a long U-turn away from us, and return to Brown Auditorium on our left (diagonally across the street from the library). The ceremony was scheduled for two o'clock; it was then ten of two. We could not have planned our visit any better. We talked with the graduate's husband as guests hurried into the auditorium. A small number of people waited outside for the processional as we did, some with cameras in hand.

Soon he said, "Here they come." Quickly I took a picture of the student marshal, Dennis Kingery, who was student council president-elect; the president of the college, Dr. Paul Hoffman, wearing the presidential silver medallion; and the commencement speaker, Dr. Leland Lengel, professor of history and politics, all smiling for the camera. The faculty and graduates followed, looking serious, some adjusting their tasseled caps.

"Quickly I took a picture of the student marshal, Dennis Kingery, who was student council president-elect; the president of the college, Dr. Paul Hoffman, wearing the presidential silver medallion; and the commencement speaker, Dr. Leland Lengel, professor of history and politics, all smiling for the camera."

Once they were all inside Brown Auditorium, John, Lib, Paul, and I walked into the lobby of the auditorium seeking brochures about the college. There an extensive and impressive student exhibit of art and pottery brought oohs and ahs from us. We also picked up printed materials about the college.

I couldn't resist climbing some wide stairs to the balcony, where I entered the heights of the darkened auditorium. The audience members seated on the balcony and on the main floor were in darkness. All lights were focused on the stage. I looked toward that lighted stage. Dignitaries sat on the left, diplomas on a wooden table at center stage. All looked ready. I knew the tremendous amount of detail that was attended to by the college marshals, registrars, and others behind the scenes to successfully orchestrate the event that was about to begin.

The president welcomed everyone. He announced that a senior would give the invocation and another senior would sing a solo. Paul, John, and Lib stood at the rear of the balcony with me as well as a number of other people. Fascinated, we stayed for the invocation and part of the solo. Then we left quietly in the darkness, knowing we had many miles to go that day to reach Dodge City.

It was 2:25 P.M. as we moved out of the parking lot at McPherson College. It took me quite a while to settle down. I had been part of the familiar academic environment again!

McPherson College impressed us with its well-maintained campus, its student/faculty ratio of ten to one, and its friendly atmosphere. That day, 81 students were graduating from about a 400-member student body. I wondered how they maintained their faculty and facilities with such a small enrollment.

We marveled, too, that we had found McPherson College without knowing its address and that it happened to be on commencement day, to boot!

Slowed down by a large roadside sign that said "Whoa!" we pulled into Gunsmoke Campground, Dodge City, Kansas, at 5:56 P.M. under sunny skies. I felt akin to the person who decided on the wording for that sign because I often said "Whoa" when I had to stop suddenly or saw that Paul needed to stop the car or motorhome quickly. This habit came from growing up around horses that plowed and pulled wagons on a dairy farm.

We had traveled 222 miles that exciting Sunday with its visits to the Eisenhower Center and McPherson College and had reached our goal of Dodge City.

Following supper in our individual coaches, Lib and I walked the dusty roads of the campground for exercise. Meanwhile, John and Paul sat at the picnic table at our campsite. They looked unsuccessfully through the printed materials that came with John's motorhome for the cruise control schematic (wiring diagram). They wanted to learn why the cruise control had stopped working when John talked on the CB. John and Paul had hooked the CB to a fuse for a battery that didn't also supply voltage to the cruise control, and the cruise control seemed to be working fine that day.

"Whether that had anything to do with it, I'm not 100 percent sure," Paul said. Paul was adept at reading electrical circuit

"Meanwhile, John and Paul sat at the picnic table at our campsite. They looked unsuccessfully through the printed materials that came with John's motorhome for the cruise control schematic (wiring diagram)."

schematics and following the lines drawn to find the source of trouble. Without a schematic of the cruise control, however, he could only guess that all was now well.

Later Paul checked the air in our tires, including the spare, with a tire air gauge. He cleaned the dirt and dust off the headlights and taillights and then went next door to talk with Lib and John about the next morning's plans. We would meet at 8:45 A.M. and sightsee in Dodge City, especially the part sometimes called Old Dodge City.

It rained during the early morning on Monday, May 22, but by the time we all piled into the tow car, the sun shone. Even so, we wore long pants and sweaters or jackets for our morning tour of Dodge City, not only the "wickedest" but also the windiest city in the United States, according to a Kansas travel guide.

Laughing and talking, with John at the wheel of the Honda, we rode from the campground to the Boot Hill Museum downtown. Founded in 1947, the museum preserves and interprets the history of Dodge City. Located on the original site of the Boot Hill Cemetery, the museum's exhibits and buildings invite visitors to go back to the

1870s as they tour the complex, which includes a cemetery and reconstructed businesses, stores, schools, and homes of Old Dodge City.

In the visitor center we paid an admission fee and watched a short film that provided a history of the town. Dodge City was founded in 1872 just west of Fort Dodge, a military post. Buffalo hunters, travelers, and the railroad assured the town's existence. By the late 1800s, Front Street in Dodge City was wild with saloons serving cattlemen, soldiers, settlers, buffalo hunters, railroad men, and mule skinners—to the benefit of card sharks and brothel keepers. It was during this time that Wyatt Earp and Bat Masterson, among others, tried to maintain peace for the sake of the respectable people in the area.

From the visitor center, we followed a self-guided tour that led us uphill on a boardwalk to the Boot Hill Cemetery. It had been used mainly for buffalo hunters, drifters, and others in the 1800s who had no family in the area. It was named for a gunman killed there and buried with his boots on. All of the human remains were moved to a new cemetery after the Boot Hill Cemetery was closed in 1879, but the site and duplicated grave markers gave the look and feel of the real cemetery and its rugged era.

It was a historical, sacred place. I thought of the people who had died and of their families back East, who probably never knew what happened to their loved ones.

Remaining on the hill, we entered the Boot Hill Building, where indoor exhibits presented the real Old West without the glamour that movies gave it. Authentic, original cowboy clothes; Winchester® and Remington rifles and Colt® pistols; and furnishings from stores and homes took me back to those times. The reproduction of a sod house captured the closed-in, gloomy sense of living there.

When Paul and I traveled westward earlier by a more southerly route, I had high hopes of seeing real cowboys. We did see some present-day cowboys and watched them perform in a rodeo at San Antonio, Texas. But the museum and village at Dodge City gave us a realistic glimpse of the old days in the West.

Leaving the Boot Hill Building and walking downhill from the cemetery, we reached a wide, level boardwalk. On one side of it, facing Front Street, was a mélange of reconstructed historic buildings of Dodge City as it was in 1876, including the Long Branch Saloon, the same saloon featured in the *Gunsmoke* television series. Ordinarily, I'm not a saloon client, but there, immersed in the history and romance of the Old West, I wanted to "taste" it all! And so in the Long Branch Saloon, I cozied up to the bar and sipped sarsaparilla from a fat, white plastic souvenir cup printed with the Boot Hill Museum and Long Branch Saloon logos on opposite sides. The cost: $1. John bought one also; he called the plastic cup with its insignias a collectible.

We wandered through many reconstructed stores, including a dry goods store, a barbershop, a gunsmith shop, a drugstore, several other saloons, and a restaurant. Other buildings and exhibits included a one-room schoolhouse, a railroad depot, a 1903 Santa Fe locomotive, a blacksmith and wheelwright shop, and a threshers' cook shack, all relocated from their original sites to the Boot Hill Museum. We concluded our visit with a tour of the Hardesty House, built in 1878 and typical of a middle-class Victorian Kansas home in the 1800s.

Not far from the Boot Hill Museum, automobiles parked facing the curb on the wide main street of present-day Dodge City. Seeing that layout, I easily envisioned whinnying horses tied to hitching posts and pioneers' wagons raising dust as they came to town for supplies.

Leaving downtown Dodge City, we drove over brick streets in a residential area, which gave the area an inviting atmosphere.

I didn't want to leave Dodge City with its Wild West history now tamed by time, but we had other eras to examine and places to ferret out farther west in Colorado, our goal for that day's travel. In particular, Miramont Castle, near Colorado Springs, intrigued me. It was said to have been built into the side of a mountain by a priest. Having read about it in a tour guidebook, I questioned how a building

"On one side of it, facing Front Street, was a mélange of reconstructed historic buildings of Dodge City as it was in 1876, including the Long Branch Saloon, the same saloon featured in the Gunsmoke *television series."*

big enough to be called a castle could be built into the side of a mountain, and by a priest at that.

The museum at Dodge City enlarged my vision of the Wild West and what those times must have been like. A thriving, law-abiding city with a population of approximately 21,000 today, Dodge City continues to be a hub for shipping cattle and a trading center for wheat grown in the region, its former "wickedness" now used to fascinate visitors.

Back at the campground after our two-hour visit to the Boot Hill Museum, we prepared to leave immediately for Colorado. We'd have lunch somewhere on the road ahead.

7

Miramont Castle

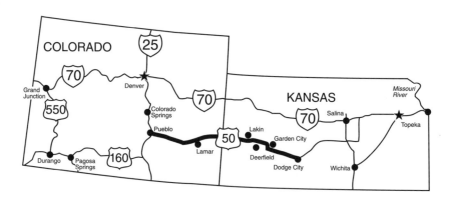

RETURNING to the Gunsmoke Campground from our eye-opening morning visit to Old Dodge City that Monday, John rehitched the tow car to his motorhome. Both he and Paul unhooked our RVs from water and electricity. We pulled away at 11:37 A.M. under sunny skies and headed on U.S. 50 toward Pueblo, Colorado, 294 miles west. From a campground there, we planned to sightsee in the area around Colorado Springs, including the beautiful chapel at the United States Air Force Academy and the Miramont Castle.

"Nice road," Paul said about U.S. 50. "Good as any interstate." The road was just two lanes wide, but it was smooth. "Not bumpety-bump like the interstates," I replied.

In western Kansas, instead of the floodwaters we encountered in Missouri, we saw low, rolling hills with grazing beef cattle as well as huge, level fields of soil that were plowed and planted with wheat, alfalfa, and corn.

Feed yards shared their distinctive aroma as we moved past. We were driving through a major cattle-raising area.

"Real country air," John said over the CB.

"That feedlot consists of 100 acres maybe," Paul said about one as we passed it. I saw an enormous confluence of beef cattle in several connecting corrals. John said the cattle were held in those fenced-in areas and fattened for market. The corrals resembled our barnyard on the farm from which my father hauled manure and spread it on our fields for fertilizer. Those fields produced bountiful crops of corn, wheat, barley, and alfalfa hay. As a tourist passing through Kansas, however, I knew little about the modern-day beef cattle industry.

I was to learn later that beef cattle raising included three steps: (1) calves nurse from beef cows and eat pasture grass the first 6 to 8 months; (2) during the next 6 to 12 months, weaned calves are fed mostly high-quality roughage or excellent grass or other plants; and (3) for the next 3 to 5 months, the yearlings are kept in a confinement feedlot and fed high-energy rations that have added protein, vitamins, and minerals. The slaughter weight, an average of 1,100 pounds, comes at about age 18 to 24 months.

Having grown up on a dairy farm with 15 to 20 cows grazing in a large, green meadow, I was not prepared to see the huge aggregation of cattle in the dark brown feedlots. No doubt, the cattle we saw had already spent time leisurely grazing on the range and were now being fattened for market.

A dairy farm in the 1930s, I was discovering, was quite different from beef cattle ranches in the 1990s. The cows on our farm each had a name, such as Bluey, and moved freely in the meadow munching green grass. As they entered the barn at milking time, each knew which was her stall. They ate "chop" (a mixture of ground grain) and switched their tails to ward off flies as we sat on three-legged stools to milk them. That was a different era, of course, and a different kind of cattle.

Later, I would remember that in a scene reminiscent of the confinement feedlots—but on a smaller scale—we would let our dairy cows out of the barn into the barnyard during the milder days of winter. My father would toss hay over the barnyard wall for them to munch on, and they could wander over to the opposite side of the yard to a watering trough for a drink. I didn't pay attention at the time, but they must have stood around in the barnyard until it was milking time. Perhaps it was the large scale of the beef cattle operations in Kansas that startled me.

We passed a sign: "Welcome to Garden City." A city of about 24,000, it was located on the Arkansas River. I noticed in a travel guide that Garden City held its annual Beef Empire Days in early June. We were too early for this 12-day celebration of the beef industry that included cowboy poetry and a Western art show.

Well past our usual time for lunch, we pulled into a shopping mall at Garden City at 12:40 P.M. While I fixed sandwiches for our lunch, Paul walked to a Radio Shack store where he bought an auto lighter extension cord so that we could plug our cellular telephone into the cigarette lighter of the motorhome. The longer cord allowed more flexibility to find a convenient place to set our bag-type telephone (a cellular telephone with a large battery, both of which are enclosed in a black leather envelope-style bag) with its four-foot cord.

Not lingering long for lunch, we left the mall at 1:16 P.M. and continued on U.S. 50 toward Lakin, Kansas. We passed another enormous feedlot.

Moments later, Paul pointed out another feedlot on the right.

"My goodness!" I could hardly believe the scene in those feeding barnyards. I saw dark mud and muck patterned with hoofprints. Cattle ate from troughs or stood idle.

Yet another large feedlot loomed into view on the right.

I knew that there are 250 million people to feed in the United States and that cattle farmers were doing their best to feed them. I had been taught that just as vegetables, such as corn and tomatoes, provide essential nutrients, so do certain meat products.

Beef contains iron, for example. When I recently tried a no-beef diet, my body became deficient in iron to the point where a doctor put me on a regimen of iron tablets. That's why I always include plenty of beef in my diet.

Our two motorhomes and one tow car continued moving westward on U.S. 50 toward Pueblo, Colorado.

"Looks like it covers the whole hillside," Paul said of another tremendous feed yard. Cattle blanketed the area. They appeared calm.

Along with the sizable feed yards in southwestern Kansas, enormous stretches of green and brown fields lay beneath a spacious sky. I felt like I would have needed long, long arms to reach the sky.

We stopped in Deerfield, Kansas, to fill up both the Graybeals' Pinnacle and our Holiday Rambler® with gasoline. Paul tries to keep our gas tank at least one-fourth full at all times, and if we're in an area where gasoline stations are few and far between, he maintains the tank at more than half full.

During that stop, I envisioned having a block of time at the computer to concentrate on what I wanted to write. Instead, twice I had to undo my computer desk, once to move the motorhome forward so that the gas pump hose would reach the motorhome gasoline tank inlet and once to unlock the driver's door for Paul. As I re-established my writing desk again, a truck pulled out of the station, sending a cloud of dust toward the open driver's door. I quickly closed the lid of the laptop computer. Modern technology brings its own frustrations.

Paul returned to the motorhome and handed the sales slip to me to record in the log and calculate our miles per gallon: only 7.903 miles per gallon.

From the gas station, we continued driving on U.S. 50 in Kansas, through Lakin and toward Pueblo, Colorado.

As I sat in the passenger seat, one end of a polished pine board about 8 inches by 20 inches lay on my lap and the other end rested just inside the glove compartment with that lid, which was hinged at the top, gently closed against it. The board made a bridge on which the laptop computer sat. Without the board, the computer was too close to my body for my fingers to work the keyboard comfortably. Occasionally I had to slide the board farther back in the glove compartment as the vibration of the road shook the board toward me. Otherwise, the board eventually would fall from its glove compartment ledge. Some later model motorhomes have computer desks built into the dashboard or provided as separate desks.

The greatest problem with using my laptop computer was having to turn it on and use a floppy disk to boot it up every writing session. This process took a lot of time. If I had a thought I wanted to save when I was not already at the computer, I usually jotted it in my spiral-bound tablet. Newer laptop computers have a "suspend" mode that allows an operator to start using the computer more quickly. They also have much more disk space so that floppy disks are unnecessary except for backup purposes.

John came on the CB to say he had heard on the radio that there was a tornado warning for all of western Kansas. It was 2:52 P.M. and we were about seven miles from the Colorado border.

We crossed the border into Colorado about three o'clock, relieved to be out of the tornado warning area and thankful that we had not encountered a twister.

We continued to gasp at the sizes of the feed yards we saw.

"Looks like it covers the whole hillside," Paul said of one at the edge of Lamar, a small town that housed a welcome center for Colorado.

We decided to stop—we especially wanted visitor information about Colorado. Inside the center's renovated Santa Fe Railroad Depot, two friendly women answered our questions about sights to see in the Colorado Springs area. As I left, I clutched a handful of colorful brochures selected from the racks.

Back in our motorhomes, we headed for Pueblo, our goal for that day. Other feed yards appeared on the right and left of U.S. 50, some huge, some small. John and Paul pulled into a rest area to let a truck and some cars pass us that had unintentionally convoyed in back of us. Courteous motorhome drivers pull off the road where there is sufficient space if two or three drivers are following close behind and there is no passing lane.

After 294 miles, at 6:00 p.m. on that sunny Monday evening, we settled in at the KOA Pueblo, Colorado, paying for two nights.

Its young deciduous trees and small shrubs made the campground an oasis in the surrounding hills of prairie grass and sagebrush. I-25 went past the campground about 300 feet away, but it was elevated and we scarcely heard the traffic noise.

For our evening meal, I used the microwave to cook the last two commercially frozen dinners from our stash in the refrigerator/freezer. Our supply of skim milk was getting low. After six days on the road, we needed to restock groceries.

Paul walked outside around the immediate area; he likes to be aware of his surroundings. Naturally curious, he chatted with other RVers on topics of similar interest during his stroll of the campground.

Fatigue creeps up on me when I travel. All of a sudden, I need extra sleep. Come to think of it, that pattern applies to my whole life. I go and go until I have to stop and sleep awhile. That evening, knowing we had finally reached Colorado and would stay in one campground for a few days, and feeling sleepy, I lay down early on the bed in the rear of the motorhome for a nap. A half-hour later, I got up and lounged on the sofa watching television, but my eyelids would hardly stay open. I decided to go to bed early. What I wasn't aware of at the time was the effect that the high altitude was having on me. In fact, I wasn't even aware that the elevation of Pueblo is 4,690 feet. At home, our elevation is only 700 feet.

In six days we had driven from the East to the West. Our tour of Colorado had begun.

On a cold, rainy, Tuesday morning, May 23, John drove Lib, Paul, and me in the Honda to Colorado Springs, about 45 minutes north of our campground on I-25. It would be our first full day in Colorado.

Colorado Springs had been the site of the Annual Conferences of our Church of the Brethren in 1931, 1948, and 1953.

First on the docket, we found Chapel Hill Mall, where Lib spotted the outside entrance to a JCPenney® hair salon. A young woman in the salon shampooed and blow-dried my hair. I had no appointment, of course, but luckily most mall hair salons welcome walk-in clients and can usually accommodate them without much waiting. While John went to Walgreen's, Lib shopped in Penney's, and Paul scouted the mall. They all regrouped at the hairdresser's.

Then we drove a few miles north of Colorado Springs on I-25 to the United States Air Force Academy, the state's most frequently visited man-made attraction.

Using a map we received from the visitor center in Lamar, where we had stopped the day before, we wound our way through 19,200 acres to the academy's visitor center.

Ducking inside the center out of the cold rain, we scouted the gift shop until the next showing of *The Pursuit of Excellence*. The 15-minute film, shown every half-hour, emphasized the honor code of the academy. Because teamwork is essential in military actions, individuals must know they can depend on one another. How great the world would be if everyone lived by such a code of ethics.

The four of us, along with a crowd of other chattering visitors, moved individually among the displays of copious items in the gift shop. Suddenly a piece of satiny black, smooth sculpture caught my eye. It was in a display of regional Native American art. A deep memory stirred within me. It stretched back to a time when I was 10 years old. My pulse quickened as I wondered if I could be in the same area of the country where my former pen pal lived. My heart felt warm and alive as my eyes searched the sculptures on display and the identifying cards of the sculptors. I wanted desperately to remember my pen pal's name, and I thought the cards might furnish a clue.

My fifth-grade teacher, Miss Callahan, at New Windsor Elementary School gave her class the names and addresses of American Indian children with whom we could be pen pals. As I remember, mine was a Pueblo girl from New Mexico. The name Pueblo stuck in my mind because we had studied about the adobe houses in which Pueblo Indians in the Southwest lived.

After several letters between us, one day I got in the mail a brown paper package, carefully wrapped, from my pen pal. Inside was a small, satin-finished, black clay animal that looked like a dachshund but was probably a horse. It was about five inches long and about three inches high. I still remember the smooth, cool feel of the clay. She had made it herself and expressed regret that it did not turn out better. To me, it was a treasure.

For years I kept her letters and the clay horse in my own special wooden drawer of the built-in wall cupboard in the dining room on the farm. When my father died from a streptococcus infection (shortly before penicillin was available), my mother had a public sale. She, my three sisters, and I moved off the farm and in with my mother's parents. The horse and letters moved with me. But in subsequent years, they became lost and I have no memory of their final days with me.

Perhaps in our explorations in Colorado I might find a clue to her identity. If not, perhaps my thoughts of her might somehow reach out to her and tell her that I still think of her kindness to me and of the memorable work of her young mind and hands.

We left the visitor center for a tour of the famous Cadet Chapel. The religious emphasis at the academy surprised and impressed me. Also impressive was the 17-spired, unique architecture of the chapel. Inside I walked in awe down the aisle of the soaring sanctuary toward the Protestant altar. The slanted stained-glass windows on each side met in apexes high above my head. The whole magnificent, yet intimate, milieu led my thoughts to God.

On the ground level, worship areas for Roman Catholics and Jews revealed the academy's respect for each person's religious beliefs. Those sacred spaces contained meaningful religious symbols and furnishings appropriate to each faith group.

Leaving the academy grounds, we ate our main meal in a nearby family restaurant, then drove south on I-25 to the Garden of the Gods, a 1,300-acre park with a visitor center. We elected to forgo the center

"Inside [the United States Air Force Academy Cadet Chapel] I walked in awe down the aisle of the soaring sanctuary toward the Protestant altar . . . The whole magnificent, yet intimate, milieu led my thoughts to God."

this time and to drive on our own into the park.

It was misty and rainy, not a good hair day, so I stayed inside the car while the others walked around outside. Like a wondering child, I sat in there looking up at towering pinnacles of red sandstone rock. I stretched my neck and peered up and up, marveling at the terra cotta–colored monuments that had been softened and embossed by wind, rain, and snow. I thought of God, his majesty, his power, and his great vision in creating such formations.

We drove on farther into the park where we saw the famous Balanced Rock, of which John took a picture. From inside the car, I strained to gaze and continued to marvel at the awesome monuments in front of and around us.

Less than one-fourth mile north from the Garden of the Gods, we drove through the grounds of Glen Eyrie, the former estate of General William Jackson Palmer, the founder of Colorado Springs and builder of the Denver and Rio Grande Railroad. The 67-room, Tudor-style castle is owned by The Navigators, an interdenominational Christian organization. The property serves as their U.S. and international

*"We drove on farther into the park [Garden of the Gods] where we saw
the famous Balanced Rock, of which John took a picture."*

headquarters. The group offers year-round tours of the castle as well
as conferences, seminars, and spiritual retreats.

Proceeding to U.S. 24, John chauffeured us to Manitou Springs,
a small town of 4,500 located at the foot of Pikes Peak. Clouds and
mist shrouded the peak. Perhaps the next day would be sunny and
we could see that famous landmark.

John found Miramont Castle, which was located at 9 Capitol Hill
Avenue off Ruxton Avenue. I could see that the castle was indeed
cozied up to the side of a mountain. As I had hoped, the exterior
looked like a castle with nine styles of architecture and greenstone
facing. Instead of a moat, it was protected by a steep hillside in front
that offered limited parking. We were glad we were in the tow car for
there would not have been room for our motorhomes.

The Manitou Springs Historical Society had restored and refur-
nished the castle and made it into a museum. When we entered by
the main front door on the first level of the four-story castle, we paid
an admission fee and received a pamphlet to use during a self-guided
tour.

"From inside the car, I strained to gaze and continued to marvel at the awesome monuments in front of and around us." [In the end, the wonder of the Garden of the Gods drew me outside the car where I captured the moment with my camera.]

We climbed stairs to begin our tour of the castle, which had been built in the late 1800s. Father Jean Baptist Francolon, a wealthy Catholic priest born in France, designed the castle and commissioned Angus Gillis, a Scottish contractor, to build it. The castle was the private home of the priest and his mother, a widow. Of the 46 rooms, they used only 28. In the Victorian era, it was popular to own a house with unusual-shaped rooms, thus most of those in the castle were anything but four-sided. The guest bedroom, for example, had 16 sides. We counted them.

Built about 1895 into the side of a mountain, the castle had no exterior back walls or windows. Its architectural styles include Romanesque, English Tudor, and Byzantine.

"Look at that!" I said just as Lib also gasped at a huge rock fireplace in the drawing room. Its 400,000 pounds rested on the solid rock of the mountain. Over the fireplace, the original African mahogany siding-type shingles covered the area from mantel to ceiling. Wood pillars in the large room had been stained to match the shingles. Opposite the fireplace was a square grand piano with rosewood veneer. The walls of the drawing room were Victorian red, a dark red that was popular during that era.

The four of us moved along with other visitors through the various rooms on each level. I compared the tiny rooms in the fourth-floor servants' quarters with the grand bedroom suite of the lady of the castle on the third floor.

The castle-museum also housed in its former basement the International Museum of Miniatures, which was filled with wonderful collections of antique toys and dolls as well as miniature houses with furniture and accessories.

On the way home, we stopped at Albertson's, where Paul and I bought milk and frozen dinners. Lib also bought the groceries she needed.

Back at the KOA Pueblo, on a cloudy evening, we ate a supper of sandwiches. Paul washed the few dishes and I dried them. I wrote a letter and postcards, and we both watched a little television. Then, tired from the day's excursions, Paul went to bed early and so did I. It had been a full, first tour day in Colorado—the United States Air Force Academy, Garden of the Gods, Glen Eyrie, and Miramont Castle. I had been impressed by the castle's architecture, but I never did find out *why* the priest had built such a large residence.

Contrary to my expectations when I started out on the trip, I was finding a lot of the Western cowboy milieu, the kind of environment I had hoped to find on our first trip from Maryland to Arizona and didn't. In the brochures that I picked up at the Lamar visitor center, I read about the ProRodeo Hall of Fame and Museum of the American Cowboy. I hoped the others would be willing to visit that attraction before we left the area.

8

ProRodeo
Hall of Fame

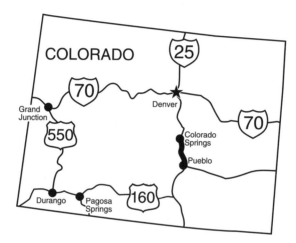

I WAS READY well before departure time
and writing at the computer (while sitting on two sofa cushions) at
the dinette table in our motorhome parked at the KOA in Pueblo,
Colorado. That Wednesday, May 24, we planned to see Royal Gorge,
which boasted the world's highest suspension bridge—1,053 feet
above the Arkansas River. John had also mentioned Seven Falls as a
place to go. I, of course, wanted to visit the ProRodeo Hall of Fame
and Museum of the American Cowboy.

Paul looked dashing in his new navy blue Savane wrinkle-free
cotton trousers and his white, short-sleeved cotton knit shirt with a
design of small black and green medallions. (He's allergic to poly-

ester.) He completed his outfit with his pricey black Hanover boots. He was ready for the day, he said.

My navy pants were topped by a rose-and-navy-blue-flowered, short-sleeved knit top. I wore my ever-faithful white canvas loafers that could be easily slipped on and off.

Before we left the campground that morning, Paul went to the office to pay for two more nights, which would make four nights at KOA Pueblo. Meanwhile, I turned off and closed the computer and wrote a note on a birthday card that I had brought from home especially for a church friend. His birthday, I was surprised to realize, was the next day! I had not looked at my calendar the last few days.

When Paul returned to the motorhome he carried a newspaper. *The Pueblo Chieftain* for that day was headlined "Senate rejects Gramm tax-cut proposal." Another front-page story declared, "Blast brings back bombing memories, helps healing begin." A photograph showed tearful reactions of people watching the implosion demolition of the Murrah Federal Building in Oklahoma City.

Soon the four of us rode in the tow car toward Royal Gorge Bridge, first on I-25 and then U.S. 50. It was beginning to dawn on me that we indeed would travel on the world's highest suspension bridge. Each one of us knew friends or family members who knelt or lay down in the back of the car and would not look out the windows because of their fear of crossing any bridge. I wondered how such talk might affect our driver, John, who appeared as steady as a rock from my vantage point behind him in the back seat. To be on the safe side, however, after some hesitation I laughingly suggested that we think positive thoughts about crossing the bridge. Putting myself in the driver's place, I remembered times when I had to focus hard on what I was doing so that fears did not panic me.

When we arrived at Royal Gorge Bridge, I looked ahead and could see the height and depth of the rugged, colorful chasm. It left me holding my breath. Between our car and the bridge were gift shops and other tourist buildings and a tollbooth. The whole place bustled with people. Royal Gorge Bridge is part of a 360-acre park operated with private funds. One pays the toll, of course, for the thrill of crossing the bridge—$8 each for senior citizens.

Leaving the tollbooth, John drove slowly down a slope, then actually moved onto the wood-planked bridge. There was no turning back. Bumpety, bumpety, bumpety. We went no faster than 10 miles per hour, the speed limit.

On both sides of our car, people *walked* on the narrow bridge! In front, a trolley set on wheels instead of tracks moved slowly, like a shepherd leading us across. When I dared to glance down, the Arkansas River looked like a gray shoelace far below.

After a long minute or so, we reached the other side. My confidence about our safety suddenly returned. Ahead of us were a café and other eateries, a theater, a craft store, and an entertainment gazebo. John found a parking place for the car. We found rest rooms, then learned that an orientation film would start in 20 minutes in the theater. To fill the time, we climbed the nearby steep, winding path to the Point Sublime gazebo. It was an open-sided, rectangular structure sitting high on a precipice overlooking the gorge.

Unusual for me, I worked at breathing as I climbed and stopped to rest several times. The altitude was about 6,000 feet.

"This is as far as I'm going, Paul. You go on. I'll meet you back at the theater." I couldn't believe I had to stay behind. After encouraging me to follow, Paul moved up the mountain.

Standing still and resting, I took deep breaths.

"It's more level once you get up here," Paul called down to me. And so I slowly, step by step, ascended again.

Finally reaching the leveler area, I entered the Point Sublime gazebo and leaned out. The thin, gray river rushed far, far below. A long train moved like a caterpillar along its edge. High above the water, tiny toylike figures walked on the suspension bridge. Off in the distance, the sun brightened flat upland meadows and wide fields. The view was spectacular up and down the gorge. To my left were fields; straight ahead and to my right were magnificent, craggy, stratified rocks. Behind me, a paved road allowed people to drive cars from the bridge up to Point Sublime where the four of us were.

*"I entered the Point Sublime gazebo [at Royal Gorge Bridge] and leaned
out. The thin, gray river rushed far, far below. A long train moved like
a caterpillar along its edge. High above the water, tiny toylike figures
walked on the suspension bridge. Off in the distance, the sun brightened
flat upland meadows and wide fields."*

We could not stay long on that magnificent, lofty point, however,
or we would miss the next showing of the film.

John and Lib hiked back down the trail while Paul and I descended
by the gentler, sloping road. By the time we got to the theater, the
Graybeals were already inside and had saved us seats beside them. Soon
a film began telling the history of the Royal Gorge Railroad as told by
a retired engineer of the Denver and Rio Grande Railroad.

All of us wanted to walk back across the bridge except Lib. We
discussed options of how to get the car back. In the end, Lib decided
that if she could follow the trolley across, she would drive the car.

It turned out that the trolley moved back across the bridge while
we were getting my coat from the trunk of the car, so brave Lib started
out on her own. As she drove slowly across the bridge 1,053 feet
above the river, John watched intently.

"Oh, I want to take a picture of Lib driving across the bridge," I
said. Hastily framing her car, I snapped the scene. John got a shot

also. When she was safely across, the rest of us began our own passages on the bridge.

I walked in a crisscross fashion from one side of the bridge to the other, looking up and down the gorge, breathing in its great depth, variegated colors, jagged rocks, and fast-flowing river at the bottom. Down there, a smaller suspension bridge carrying railroad tracks allowed trains to continue their trip in the deep gorge where there was no land area for tracks between the steep wall of rock and the water. Matchbox-size buildings near the river indicated where the world's steepest incline railway finished its journey down the side of the rocky chasm.

About halfway across the suspension bridge, a sign said, "This is the spot where David Kirke made his bungi-rope jump for ABC-TV's *That's Incredible*." Leaning over the railing, I took a picture of the great drop from the bridge toward the river, railroad tracks, and rugged rocks beneath.

A brisk, cool breeze blew—my fingers and nose were getting cold. Ahead of me on the bridge, Paul shouted for me to come on, that John had already crossed. I hurried to catch up.

At the end of the bridge, Lib met us saying she had taken a picture of Paul and me as we walked the last few feet of the bridge together.

What an experience! While Paul regretted that the incline railway was closed for repair, we all agreed that the 39-mile drive that morning was well worth it to see the Royal Gorge and travel on its breathtaking suspension bridge.

On our way to the car, Lib and I couldn't pass up entering a gift shop. Inside it, John asked a salesperson for the best route to Cripple Creek from Royal Gorge Bridge. We soon were following her directions to the historic gold-mining town, hoping to buy lunch there and perhaps see a melodrama and otherwise sightsee.

We drove from Royal Gorge Bridge on Route 9, a long, paved, winding road through farm valleys, and then on an unpaved local road to reach Cripple Creek. A thriving gold-mining town of 18,000 in the late 1800s, its population has diminished to 650 permanent residents. While some active gold mining is still done in the area, to our surprise, legalized gambling had come to Cripple Creek. The town had 24 casinos and its population swelled daily as buses brought in casino players.

We parked behind the Midnight Rose Hotel and Casino, the only parking lot with space available. John paid the $5 fee that the attendant said would be returned by the cashier at the Midnight Rose Casino. Inside the building adjacent to the lot, we found a restaurant and each of us ordered a New York strip steak for only $3.95. Paul's steak had a lot of gristle, so the waitress graciously and promptly brought him another. Mine was delicious, as were the mashed potatoes with brown gravy, my favorite side dish.

After eating, we wove our way through the noisy, busy gambling arena to the main street of Cripple Creek. Under cloudy skies, we walked to the Imperial Hotel to learn if the traditional Victorian melodrama was being presented. It didn't start until June. Then gift and antique stores lining the street drew us inside. At 2:36 P.M., I took a picture of the main street of historic Cripple Creek. We stopped for ice cream at Wendy's in the basement of the Midnight Rose Hotel and Casino and after John retrieved his $5 from the cashier, we left by the rear entrance.

"It's snowing," someone said. Sure enough, flurries floated about in what I had thought was merely cold, foggy weather.

On the northern edge of Cripple Creek, we passed up the opportunity to tour the Mollie Kathleen Gold Mine, 1,000 feet underground. Two in our foursome did not like caves. Anyway, we had had our share of heights and depths that day!

We left Cripple Creek on Route 67 to U.S. 24, toward Colorado Springs—a different route from the one on which we had entered. We passed through mountains and snow flurries.

Much later near Colorado Springs, off of U.S. 24, we stopped at Van Briggle Art Pottery, a world-acclaimed pottery workshop and one of the oldest still active in the United States. Since 1899, artisans have been creating beautiful vases, figurines, and lamps in art nouveau and traditional Southwestern designs with a soft matte glaze.

We took a free, interesting tour through their studios that included watching one of the artisans throw (form) a pot on a potter's wheel. In the gift shop later, Lib bought an original sculpted piece portraying a young Indian girl making bread, and I bought an original fluted bowl with a braided handle for my daughter-in-law, Nancy.

Back at the motorhome at the KOA Pueblo campground, I fixed scrambled eggs for Paul's and my supper. After doing the dishes with me, Paul decided it was time to take off his shoes and count his money. Actually, he no longer carried cash in his shoe as he had done on our earlier trips. But he did count the money he had with him.

"How much cash do you have?" he asked me. Between the two of us, he decided that if we used our credit and debit cards we would probably have enough cash for the trip, and definitely for the moment.

We enjoyed a lazy evening watching television. We never knew what television channels would be available at a campground. Mountainous terrain, location and signal strength of the transmitting station, and obstructions such as buildings could affect television reception. Some campgrounds offered cable hookups. Usually we accepted whatever channels the area offered without paying the extra charge for a cable hookup. If we were going to stay for a while and thought we would want to watch specific programs, we paid for cable service, normally about $2 extra. Some of our RVing friends have installed small, individual satellite dishes to ensure good television reception.

To use normal television, we raise the antenna that normally lays on the roof by turning a lever inside the motorhome and rotating a plastic dial to point the prongs of the antenna in the direction necessary to receive television signals. We also turn on a wall switch that supplies power to the pre-amplification component of the receiving system.

If the campground offers cable television service and we decide to use it, we simply plug one end of our coaxial cable into the source (which is usually on the same post as the electricity hookup) and the other end into the motorhome's outside receptacle. Paul carries an extra length of coaxial cable in case it is required to span the distance to the campground's source.

That day's weather had kept us entertained. Cloudy all day, at times it misted, appeared to dry out, rained, and snowed, and occasionally the sun cast shadows under trees. A newscaster said that the normal temperatures for the Pueblo area were in the low 70s, but the temperatures during our week had been an average of 30 degrees below normal.

I went to bed by 9:30, my eyelids too heavy to read or watch any more television. Sightseeing took energy but I liked it. I postponed writing in the computer, thinking I would get up early the next morning to do that.

I was up at 6:26 A.M. on Thursday and began writing at the computer at the dinette table. Ten o'clock was our departure time, a little later than usual. We planned to find Seven Falls near Colorado Springs, have lunch at the Broadmoor Hotel, and take the highway to Pikes Peak summit, weather cooperating. The ProRodeo Hall of Fame was not on our list that day.

In our motorhome, we were using two methods of heating simultaneously. The propane furnace blew warm air through floor vents. Sometimes the rig cooled down too much before the next cycle of heating began, so we plugged in a small electric cube heater that circulated warm air when its sensor detected a need for heat between furnace cycles.

The outside temperature was about 40 degrees; it was very overcast and foggy. Unless conditions changed, going up Pikes Peak would be a lost cause that day and maybe forever, what with life's uncertainties and the mountain's distance from Maryland. We planned to leave the area the next morning for Durango.

I typed steadily into the computer, reliving the previous day's awesome encounter with Royal Gorge Bridge. By 7:40 A.M. Paul was eating his breakfast of corn flakes with banana, raisins, and pieces of hard roll in milk and drinking his usual hot water with milk and sugar. It still looked foggy.

In rain at the appointed hour of 10:00, John drove us on I-25 toward Seven Falls, about an hour north of the campground. Paul and John usually sat in the front seat with Lib behind Paul and me behind John in the back seat. En route Lib wondered if we would even be able to see the falls because of the clouds and rain.

We entered the Seven Falls archway, which spanned a two-lane road, and soon exclaimed at how close the gigantic walls of rock were on either side. Down the narrow canyon in which we found ourselves rushed a trout stream on our left that also served as a water supply for Colorado Springs.

Driving farther into South Cheyenne Cañon, a sign warned us that a nearby rest room was the only one in that area. We decided to stop and found it to be a clean, modern facility.

Deeper into the canyon, we paid the senior citizen admission of $5 per person and then saw a sign warning us to turn around immediately if we did not want to assume the risks of the canyon. Although the sign did not mention specific risks, I assumed that it meant the flash flooding that can occur in such rock-bound channels. We drove ahead.

Soon we parked and walked into a cool, damp, dark tunnel 170 feet inside the mountain. An elevator carried as many as 20 passengers at a time 12 stories up, 130 feet through the mountain itself, to the Eagle's Nest Platform, only a 40-second ride. Leaving the elevator, we walked out onto a platform looking for the falls. Not seeing them, we rounded a corner of the mountain. We caught our first sight of the white-foamed, gushing Seven Falls, cascading down seven distinct levels. Each of the falls had been named; from the top to the bottom they were Ramona, Feather, Bridal Veil, Shorty, Hull, Weimer, and Hill. With Paul holding an umbrella to shield my camera from the rain, I took a picture of John and Lib with the falls in the background. Chipmunks scampered over the steep, bare rock wall beside the platform.

Of all places to have a gift shop! We browsed the tiny one at Eagle's Nest, tucked in a space not much larger than a couple of elevators. I bought five postcards for $1—a bargain. After descending in the elevator, we walked slowly this time through the 170-foot-long egress tunnel on our way out. We examined exhibits in wall cases along the sides while water occasionally dripped down on us from the ceiling.

Outside, with our umbrellas up, we walked to the base of the falls. A 224-step stairway scaled the granite wall. I read later that it led to a mile-long nature trail and overlook of Colorado Springs and the plains of eastern Colorado. Paul climbed bravely up the wet, steep, open steps ascending far enough to feel the water ravaging down, spraying him and us below with its mist.

Lib and I hurried out of the cold rain into a large gift shop on the ground level near the foot of the falls. We enjoyed its warmth. As we browsed the jewelry and clothes, Lib commented that the shop had items of high quality.

Retracing our route out of the canyon in the car, we again drew our breath at the formations of rock on either side of the narrow passageway. We learned that from mid-May to mid-September the canyon was illuminated at night with spectacular lights for visitors to see its granite walls, rock formations, and Seven Falls.

"Paul climbed bravely up the wet, steep, open steps [at Seven Falls] ascending far enough to feel the water ravaging down, spraying him and us below with its mist."

Since John and Lib were both avid golfers, our next stop was the famous Broadmoor Hotel in Colorado Springs, where the Ladies Professional Golf Association (LPGA) would hold its U.S. Open later in the year. We entered the lobby, where a desk clerk described the hotel's various dining rooms. Because of our tourist attire, we chose to eat lunch in the casual Tavern restaurant.

Afterward, we took the escalator to the Main Mezzanine. There we admired the various lobbies and peeked into the Main Ballroom. Descending by the grand staircase, we visited the Espressos Café, where John and I bought irresistible cinnamon buns. In the gift shop next door, Lib bought a box of attractive playing cards to be used as a prize at one of her bridge club meetings.

In the continuing rain, John gallantly retrieved the car and brought it to the front door. We all scrambled inside it. As we left the Broadmoor Hotel, we decided to try going up Pikes Peak, located some distance northwest. We regained I-25 and took U.S. 24 to Manitou Springs to reach the Pikes Peak Highway.

The rain had stopped and it was foggy as we optimistically drove up the paved mountain road toward Pikes Peak. Before long, a large sign at the top of a large green tollbooth with a stone foundation announced "Pikes Peak Highway." Another, smaller sign at the right-hand, front corner of the stone wall said "Information. Pay toll here. Enjoy your trip."

John parked the car in a wide paved area and walked over to the tollbooth. The person in the tollbooth told him that the road was closed at the top because it was *snowing*. When John relayed the information to us, we decided that if we couldn't go to the top, then we didn't want to spend money to go only part of the way. We didn't know what weather we might encounter farther up the mountain.

We turned around and went back down the mountain. I, for one, was disappointed, but we talked about how fortunate we were to have seen the top of magnificent Mount McKinley in Alaska's sunshine during our visit there two years earlier.

I held my breath as the four of us discussed what to do instead. To my surprise, the consensus was to see the ProRodeo Hall of Fame

"The person in the toll booth told him [John] that the road was closed at the top [of Pikes Peak] because it was snowing. . . . we decided that if we couldn't go to the top, then we didn't want to spend money to go only part of the way. We didn't know what weather we might encounter farther up the mountain."

and Museum of the American Cowboy. We retraced our earlier ride on U.S. 24, gained I-25, and drove north in Colorado Springs to exit 147.

The purpose of the ProRodeo Hall of Fame and Museum of the American Cowboy is to document through film, art, and artifacts how today's sport—and for some, the business—of rodeo competition evolved from the lifestyle of working cowboys. I felt I had "hit the jackpot" in seeing the history and trappings of cowboy life.

At the museum, the four of us watched two films at separate showings that documented the history of rodeo as well as today's rodeo lifestyle. In between the two shows, a pleasant, knowledgeable woman guided us among exhibits of cowboy gear and explained the tack, such as saddles and bridles, used in rodeos. Later in the Heritage Hall of Fame, I wandered on my own along glass cases of exhibits. They showed photographs, memorabilia, and trophies of individual cowboys whose feats and prowess earned them a place in the hall of fame.

I roamed through the exhibits and soaked up the cowboy atmosphere. I kept thinking of the risks rodeo cowboys take every time they enter a competition, how hardy they are, how unpretentious their world is. When I read of their feats of daring in unglamorous arenas, often isolated from the rest of the world, and saw their photographs, their worn boots, spurs, chaps (leather leggings), belt buckles, and coiled lariats now resting peacefully, the spirit of the cowboy reached into my mind and heart. My father, who loved cowboy stories, seemed to be there with me.

As we splashed back to the campground in the late afternoon, Lib and I napped in the back seat of the station wagon. Paul and John talked as the occasion merited. I like riding in the rain when I'm not driving.

John did an outstanding job of driving, both as leader in the motorhome and as driver of the tow car. He pointed out sights and did not mind stopping for what any of us wanted to see, even suggesting possibilities. Nor did he hurry us through exhibits. I really appreciated his graciousness and flexibility.

Back at the KOA Pueblo campground, I fixed canned vegetable soup for supper. Paul had crackers with his soup. I heated the cinnamon bun from the Broadmoor Hotel in the microwave and enjoyed it as both bread and dessert. Loaded with raisins and pecan pieces, it tasted yummy!

Paul fixed his own dessert. He can't eat a lot of sweets so he creates cereal concoctions to suit his fancy. Sometimes he adds peanut butter or raisins or ice cream or a plain sugar or butter cookie. Once when he lived at his parent's home, he even put gravy over his cereal when they had run out of milk. It's easy to cook for Paul.

The glow I felt after hearing about the history of Western cowboys and seeing their outfits stayed with me that evening. Seven Falls and the Broadmoor Hotel filled their own niches of learning and visual excitement for me, but the ProRodeo experience went much deeper into the haunts of my childhood when my father was still alive. It alone was worth the trip to Colorado.

Still, next on our itinerary was Durango, with the possibility of a ride on a narrow gauge railroad train high up into the southern range of the Rocky Mountains. I had learned that these famous mountains got their name from early 19th century explorers who were describing their rugged topography.

That Thursday evening at the Pueblo campground, because we would be leaving the campground in the morning, Paul checked the oil levels in the engine and auxiliary generator, checked to be sure our turn signals and lights were functioning properly, and made sure we had one-fourth tank of fresh water on board. Although the motorhome was connected to a sewer connection at our site at the campground, Paul did not keep the gray water (used water that drains from the kitchen and bathroom sinks and the shower into a holding tank located beneath the main floor of the RV) and black water (waste from the toilet that is flushed into the black water holding tank, also located beneath the main floor of the RV) tank valves open all the time because he had learned that the sewer hose drains more efficiently when there is a surge of water going through. In the morning, Paul would open the valves and drain both the gray and black water tanks before disconnecting the sewer hose. He usually dumps the gray and black water holding tanks about every third evening when traveling from one location to another.

Campgrounds without individual sewer connections at campsites offer a dump station. In that instance, Paul drives on the campground road to the dump station, which is basically an opening into a sewer disposal system set apart from the rest of the campground.

To dump the gray and black water tanks on our motorhome, he first puts on his leather work gloves that he keeps handy under the front driver's seat. From the outside he opens the driver's door, reaches for the gloves, and proceeds with his task.

Then he retrieves the blue coiled sewer hose from its compartment at the rear of the coach. He places the outlet end of the sewer hose into the opening at the dump station. Then from the side of the coach he reaches into its basement interior, removes a safety cap, and connects the inlet end of the sewer hose to a pipe that drains both the black and gray water tanks. He drains the black water out of its tank first and then the gray water from that tank.

When both tanks are drained, he disconnects the sewer hose from the motorhome and flushes that hose with water from a spigot furnished by the campground at the dump station. After laying the sewer hose on the ground, Paul re-attaches the safety cap to the discharge pipe from the holding tanks. Then he picks up the blue sewer hose and returns it to its storage compartment at the rear of the motorhome. He walks back to the campground spigot and, using a long-handled sprayer, washes any waste spilled on the concrete apron down into the dump station's sewer opening. He then recaps the sewer system opening. It doesn't take him long; he performs the whole procedure easily, as if he were getting gasoline at a service station.

That evening at Pueblo, when Paul came back inside, I was reclining on the sofa watching one of my favorite comedies on television. Not much interested in that, he sat at the dinette table reading the local newspaper. After watching my program, I handed the remote control to him for the remainder of the evening. We've learned to accommodate one another's wishes without getting ruffled about which program to watch.

9

Durango to Silverton by Narrow Gauge Railroad

IT WAS A FOGGY, 48-degree Friday morning when we pulled away from our campsites at the KOA Pueblo, Colorado, at eight o'clock. John and Lib again led our two-motorhome caravan. We headed south on I-25 toward Walsenberg, Colorado, where we would turn west on U.S. 160 toward Durango in southwestern Colorado, our destination for that day. From Durango, we wanted to visit the cliff dwellings at Mesa Verde National Park and, we hoped, ride a narrow gauge railroad up into the Rocky Mountains.

Paul had settled comfortably behind the wheel as we rode along in the misty air on the interstate. I reached for the laptop computer, and soon my fingers flew over the keys as I began to describe the amazing Seven Falls, the grand Broadmoor Hotel, and the soul-satisfying ProRodeo Hall of Fame, which we had seen the day before.

About ten minutes after our departure from the campground, the sun burned its way through the fog and shone brightly. It was almost an intrusion.

I paused from writing at my computer, looked at the sky, and said, "It rained Tuesday, Wednesday, and Thursday, the three days that we were in the Colorado Springs area. But we did our sightseeing anyway, except for Pikes Peak. I don't even see any clouds in the sky here."

John's voice came over the CB, "We're finally seeing the Rockies of Colorado over to the right."

Quickly dropping my gaze to the horizon on my right, I saw snowcapped mountains, their blue gray shadows contrasting with the white frosting of snow. Mist and fog had hidden them from us until that moment.

About 9:30 A.M., we turned off I-25 and drove into Walsenberg on U.S. 160. Paul pumped gasoline into the 60-gallon tank of our motorhome at the BP station. He likes to pump sufficient gasoline to fill the tank and make the cost come out to an even amount, such as $48.00 rather than $48.34. He finds not having to bother with cents less confusing later when checking the credit or debit card statements.

We then headed west on U.S. 160. Having caught up with writing about yesterday's events, I began typing into that electronic marvel my thoughts and observations on that day's trip to Durango.

A sign on the west edge of Walsenberg said that La Veta Pass was open. As an Easterner, I thought a "pass" was a low, narrow place in a road, usually between huge rocks. In cowboy movies, robbers jumped onto stagecoaches from the tops of rocks "at the pass," or Gene Autry on his horse would "cut them off at the pass."

In the West, I was to learn that the topography of a pass was different—it was a place where early travelers found it possible to get over a mountain. These days, passes are open or closed depending on whether snow prevents traveling through them. I was also to learn that sooner or later as you travel from eastern to western Colorado, you will traverse a mountain pass.

As we rode through the scenic valley toward La Veta Pass, I looked ahead at snowcapped mountains and let myself enjoy their textures, shadows, lines, shapes, positive and negative spaces, and color contrasts as an artist might. Being in the valley with its prairie grass and shrubs lying peacefully at the foot of mountains made me feel safe and warm. I thought, Dear God, I do thank you for this beautiful day and drive.

From the valley we climbed steadily and reached La Veta Summit at an altitude of 9,413 feet. As we headed downhill among the mountains, a sign informed us that far below lay San Luis Valley. From a travel guide booklet, I learned that the valley was a semi-arid plain, high in elevation and flat, about 50 miles wide and 125 miles long. An ancient lake once occupied its surface. With irrigation from the Rio Grande and artesian wells, the valley was currently one of the most productive agricultural regions in the state.

Meanwhile, having just come over the summit, Paul said, "Outside temperature has dropped 15 degrees at least," to demonstrate that high elevations affect air temperatures. We have a small thermometer mounted on the driver's side mirror that Paul can look at while driving or, if he is too busy, I can look at from behind the driver's seat.

Our climb and descent to San Luis Valley from La Veta Pass was on a comfortable, two-lane highway with shoulders (three lanes when going uphill). Clouds floated everywhere with blue sky above them. Clumps of sagebrush looked like fields of cabbages on our right and left.

As I wrote into the computer, my makeshift desk very slowly slipped away from the glove compartment. I shifted it back into place. The paved road was smooth and enjoyable.

As a courtesy to the drivers of cars and trucks behind us on the road, both John and Paul steered the motorhomes to the wide paved shoulder to allow the other vehicles to pass. Tractor-trailers were among the traffic passing us.

"Boy, such a *big* sky!" I waved my hands in a sweeping motion from center to sides. It looked like the clouds and sky enclosed us in an enormous half circle. At that location, the San Luis Valley was wide and level; distant mountains at the horizon rimmed the half circle of sky and clouds.

We entered Rio Grande County near noon and began seeing large fields newly seeded and long irrigators on wheels traveling the fields.

"There's a real cowboy! I see a real cowboy!" I exclaimed. I looked over my shoulder toward a ranch to savor the sight of a man wearing a blue shirt and dark cowboy hat and riding a reddish horse as he examined a ditch in a field across from us.

It was lunchtime when we entered Del Norte. Since we hadn't found a rest area to pull into, we parked along the side of the street, carefully choosing an area where we would not block anyone's way.

After lunch, our motorhomes and tow car climbed toward Wolf Creek Pass, elevation 10,850 feet.

"Snow squall off to the left," said Paul. Across the valley on the next mountain, I saw a white, foglike mist of snow. "Snowing here now," Paul added as flakes came toward the windshield.

"First time I've ever been in a snow squall on Memorial Day weekend," John said over the CB.

It continued to snow as we climbed slowly up the mountain, maneuvering switchbacks and curves. John and Paul talked on the CB, mostly about road and weather conditions. Paul turned on the wipers, but no snow accumulated on the road, for which I was glad.

We reached Wolf Creek Pass and began going down the steep, winding road. The falling snow thinned out and Paul put the wipers on "Intermittent."

"Isn't that pretty over here?" Paul asked, pointing to his left at snow-laden trees.

"Yeah, makes you want to get out your sled."

As we moved down the mountain, the road leveled and we passed a sign that said "End Snow Slide Area." We paused at a scenic overlook and took pictures of the green and brown valley below. During our descent from Wolf Creek Pass, the snow became rain. As we approached the valley, we admired rich, green grass covering fields and foothills. Dark green pine and deciduous trees with yellow-green, young leaves grew on the hillsides on both sides of the road.

By midafternoon, the sun was out! The Graybeals motored about 150 feet ahead of us on the road, which remained wet from the rain.

John drove slowly through the outskirts of Pagosa Springs to let faster traffic pass. On the other end of town, our small caravan continued on scenic route U.S. 160. We drove past ranches with colorful names such as Lone Elk Ranch, Yellow Jacket Ranch, and Florida Acres.

At last we reached the Durango city limits. Founded as a mining town in 1880, Durango had become a shipping center for the surrounding ranching and agricultural region as well as a major tourist attraction. It had a population of about 12,500; its elevation was 6,505 feet.

By 4:05 P.M. we pulled into Alpen Rose RV Park, two miles north of Durango. It was sunny and 58 degrees. "The fellows," as Lib called John and Paul, had driven 302 miles from the KOA Pueblo that morning. They registered for only two nights since we had not yet decided on riding the narrow gauge railroad to Silverton, which would take a day. We definitely planned to see the cliff dwellings of Mesa Verde the next day.

After eating dinner in our motorhome, Paul went outside and was soon chatting with a neighbor. It's easy to strike up conversations in campgrounds, and Paul enjoys learning something new or offering information. That evening he learned that the neighbor had bought a city transit bus that was in relatively good condition. He had taken everything out of it, raised the roof, installed full living quarters, put in either a rebuilt or new engine, and repainted the bus. Working over a period of two or three years, he had done the conversion himself at a cost of $50,000 including the bus itself. It was a handsome coach.

While Paul was outside, I totaled our expenses and mileage in the trip log and wrote some postcards. Later we both watched television. I would soon need to do laundry, but the laundry building was not very near our campsite and my motivation was feeble that evening.

At breakfast the next day, Saturday, May 27, I felt weak and shaky, lightheaded, and nauseous.

"I don't feel well."

"What do you mean?" Paul said.

"I just don't feel like myself. I wonder if I might be homesick. Maybe I should try to call Jeff and Nancy again." We had not been able to talk directly with them that trip because of schedule conflicts. I'd heard Jeff's voice on messages, but we had not had a real conversation.

Paul walked with me to the pay telephone at the office, but the telephone didn't work. We were thinking about using the cellular telephone in our motorhome but decided against it because of the high costs when roaming the country. We reserved it for emergencies.

I really wanted to see the cliff dwellings at Mesa Verde National Park that day as planned. I had looked forward to seeing them from the moment I first read about them in a tour book.

Back in the motorhome, an idea came to me. Might my sickness be related to the high altitude? Might I be suffering from what's known as "mountain sickness"? Durango's elevation was 6,500 feet, Pueblo's had been 4,690, and my hometown of Westminster, Maryland, was a mere 700 feet above sea level.

I remembered reading something about altitude sickness in one of the travel books I had picked up at the welcome center in Lamar, Colorado. Soon I found information that at elevations above 5,000 feet, the heart may beat faster and the breathing rate may increase because of the lower levels of oxygen in the air. This is normal. But I also learned that for the first two or three days at higher elevations, some people may experience dizziness, nausea, fatigue, shortness of breath, nasal congestion, headaches, and sleeping difficulties.

So the high altitude was my problem! The antidote is to take deep breaths; avoid overexertion; eat high-carbohydrate foods; go easy on alcohol, caffeine, and salty foods; and drink more water than usual. I took some long, deep breaths and began to feel better immediately.

Before leaving Durango for Mesa Verde National Park that morning, we found the railroad station and bought tickets for a train ride the next day on the Durango-Silverton Narrow Gauge Railroad.

In the tow car en route to Mesa Verde National Park on U.S. 160, occasionally I consciously breathed deeply. My confidence in being able to cope returned, but I realized that my full acclimation to the heights might take a while. The information I had read said that it would be a good idea, if possible, to stay at 5,000 feet for a day or two before going higher. I was already higher than that and I did want to continue sightseeing with the others.

Mountain sickness was *not* on my agenda. But having come from a town not very far above sea level, I was learning through experience that changes in elevation make a difference in temperature, weather, vegetation, and how well the body performs.

A few snow flurries floated in the air that Saturday morning as we walked from the car to the Far View Visitor Center in Mesa Verde National Park. Elevations range from about 6,000 feet to 8,571 feet at Park Point, the highest place in the park. Mesa Verde National Park's spring temperatures are a high of 60 degrees, a low of 34 degrees, and an average of 47 degrees along with 5.5 inches of snow.

In the visitor center, among a milling crowd near the park rangers' counter, we learned that we could choose one ranger-guided tour of either Cliff Palace or Balcony House, both cliff dwellings, but not both because of the high volume of visitors. A small fee is required for a ticket. Because the tour to Balcony House was described in our visitor guide as being quite strenuous, including crawling on hands and knees through a tunnel, we decided to see Cliff Palace, the largest and best known of the cliff dwellings in the park. Even so, that tour included a 75-foot ascent, which involved climbing steps and several short ladders. Paul bought tickets for the four of us. Since they were for an afternoon tour, we had time to meander among the exhibits and through the gift shop at the center.

The park itself is located in the high plateau country of southwestern Colorado. Mesa Verde National Park was established in 1906 and was the first national park in the United States set aside for the preservation of sites, works, and relics of prehistoric people. It is known worldwide as an interesting archeological site. In addition to the ranger-guided tours that the Graybeals and we chose, the park concessioner also offers all-morning, all-afternoon, and full-day tours. Other services of the concessioner include lodging, camping, restaurants, the visitor center, and gift shop. The park is open year-round; the concessioner accepts reservations throughout the year.

I was roaming in the gift shop when a display of satiny black pots drew me closer. Excited, I saw that their smooth finish and totally black exterior resembled my childhood pen pal's work. Her gift so long ago had given me a vibrant connection with the fine collection of Native American pots in front of me. I stood and looked at their engaging symmetry and smooth finish, all the while thanking my youthful pen pal for awakening me to the art of fine pottery.

Following lunch at the Far View Terrace near the visitor center, John once again used his excellent chauffeuring skills as we toured Ruin Road on our own, following the map in the visitor guide. We stopped at Navajo Canyon overlook and Sun Point, where we looked across a wide expanse of the semi-arid canyon to see ruins of cliff dwellings in the walls of rock beyond.

Our instructions in the visitor guide were to meet the ranger 10 minutes before the tour at the site of the tour. Tours took approximately one hour and left every half-hour.

At the appropriate time, John drove us to the Cliff Palace parking area, where we soon joined others waiting for the 2:00 P.M. tour. The butte, Mesa Verde, on which we waited covered 80 square miles and rose about 2,000 feet on its north side, its highest point above the valley. Spanish for "green table," Mesa Verde was so named because the butte is almost level and contains many juniper and pinyon trees.

While we waited for the tour to start, I stood behind a waist-high stone wall at a point on top of the mesa and looked down toward Cliff Palace. I could see that it consisted of many ecru-colored clay structures and rooms built into a large alcove in the east wall of Cliff Canyon. It faced south and southwest to capture the afternoon sunshine in cold winter months. People on a tour ahead of us looked like gnats below from where I stood.

Soon a park ranger, a retired professor, was talking with our group in the waiting area before leading us down to the actual dwellings. He told us that the Anasazi Indians built the structures we would see and occupied them for about 75 years in the 13th century. No one knows for sure why the Anasazi dwellers left, but population growth and a long drought may have caused them to move. The name Anasazi comes from a Navajo Indian word meaning "the ancient ones." Archaeologists apply the name to the prehistoric Basket Makers and the Pueblo Indians of North America.

The congenial ranger asked us to be careful as we descended a winding combination of stone steps and a narrow sloping dirt-and-rock path until we reached the level of the dwellings. Visitors had to travel in a one-way traffic pattern: they descended to the very limited space on the cliff, moved along in front of the dwellings, left the dwelling area at the far end by climbing up steep steps and ladders, and then reached the top of the mesa.

I took a picture of Lib and John just before we made our way across the precipice in front of Cliff Palace, the largest cliff dwellings in the world. Cliff Palace has approximately 100 rooms and 23 kivas (ceremonial structures); it housed about 100 people.

The circular-shaped kivas intrigued us. Originally, when they had their roofs, they could be used for ceremonial events or as good places for daily social activities, a forerunner of the family room in my mind. The doorless rooms were entered by climbing through a hatch in the roof and down a ladder.

One person in our group asked how the Anasazi people got their water. We learned that no springs or streams had been found nearby. If there had once been some, they had dried up. It was thought that

"Cliff Palace has approximately 100 rooms and 23 kivas (ceremonial structures); it housed about 100 people."

the cliff dwellers had to make a long walk across the canyon for water. In addition, the dwellers had to climb up and down ladders or steep rocky steps to reach the top of the butte to do their farming.

My admiration for those people grew as I contrasted their arduous lifestyle with the comforts and conveniences that we take for granted.

At the conclusion of the tour, I let others go ahead before I began the 75-foot climb on ladders up a narrow passageway to reach the top of the butte. Moving slowly, I stopped several times just to breathe deeply. Even children sounded winded at the top. When I finally stepped onto the mesa, I found Lib and John looking as if they were glad to rest sitting on a nearby log bench as they waited for Paul and me.

Instead of going directly back to the campground in Durango, we traveled farther west to Cortez, looking for a jewelry store called Notah-Dineh Trading Company, at 345 West Main Street. Lib learned of it while talking with someone at the visitor center in Mesa Verde National Park.

Notah-Dineh offered an extensive display of Native American art, crafts, jewelry, and heirlooms. Lib found a beautiful liquid silver

"At the conclusion of the tour [of Cliff Palace at Mesa Verde National Park], I let others go ahead before I began the 75-foot climb on ladders up a narrow passageway to reach the top of the butte."

(tiny particles of silver strung together into a fine, flexible, soft-feeling strand that shimmers and moves delicately) necklace and matching earrings. For my daughter-in-law's birthday, I also selected a liquid silver necklace and earrings with an intricate and delicate weave pattern by a Native American artisan. After shopping on the main floor, we went downstairs to see the adjoining museum of Old West and Native American artifacts, which fascinated us.

Back in Durango, we stopped for dinner at a local steakhouse and enjoyed chatting with a young couple sitting at the next table who formerly lived in Maryland. We shopped for some groceries en route to our camping sites.

When we returned to the campground, the Graybeals and we moved our RVs to a couple of new sites. When we first registered, we had said we wanted sites with water and electricity. The campground registrar had given them to us but asked that we move to different sites the next day to accommodate a large group coming in.

I had had an exciting, fulfilling day of being in touch with history and some of its ancient people. The laundry would have to wait another day, even though the laundry building was then conveniently nearby at our new site.

Something told me to take along pillows and an extra sweater for our train ride to Silverton the next day, Sunday, May 28. The day before, the ticket agent at the train station had said the heat had been turned off in the train cars for the summer. Our tickets guaranteed us reserved seats in a closed car, but someone might want to open a window.

So, carrying a shopping bag stuffed with two small sofa pillows, a sweater, and my usual handbag and camera and wearing my long blue London Fog raincoat over a blue sweat suit, I joined Paul, Lib, and John for an early morning car ride to the station in Durango. Our train was scheduled to leave at 8:30 A.M., but we were told to be there by 7:30 A.M.

Our gold souvenir tickets described the train excursion as "A Trip to Yesterday on the Narrow Gauge Silverton Train from Durango, Colo. to Silverton, Colo., and Return via D. & S.N.G. Railroad." We were in car number 10, seats 27 and 28. Paul gave me the window-seat ticket; he had the aisle-seat ticket.

As we milled around with countless other potential train riders in the railroad station, an announcer said that two trains would be leaving; ours would leave at 8:45 instead of 8:30. Apparently, so many tourists wanted to ride the train that the railroad had to add a second run.

When our turn came, we climbed aboard a black metal platform at the end of yellow train car number 10 and soon entered a no-frills train car. Our small pillows immediately spared us from the cold vinyl cushion seats. I learned later that steam/coal trains must use vinyl because coal smoke produces soot that damages fabric seats.

The train slowly pulled out of the station and chugged through the town of Durango. It headed for the mountains and Silverton, population 700, elevation 9,032 feet. Buttercups and dandelions bloomed alongside the tracks. As we rounded curves, I saw the coal-fired, steam locomotive emitting white and gray moist billows into the cool outside air.

Passengers chatted as they looked at the whitecaps in the Animas River flowing beside the tracks. They exclaimed about places where the tracks perched high above rocky gorges.

John and Lib sat behind us. In front were a couple with their three children from Moberly, Missouri, whom we enjoyed meeting.

The day's trip would take approximately nine hours. The train ran along a 45-mile course from Durango to Silverton, stopped for two hours to allow passengers to eat and explore that historic town, and returned to Durango. Silverton is the seat of San Juan County; it is in the San Juan National Forest, which lies in the San Juan mountain range. It is a 19th-century silver-mining town that originally was named Baker's Park. Its name was changed when mines nearby produced silver by the ton, some $65 million worth. Today the tourist trade maintains it, thanks in large measure to the Durango and Silverton Narrow Gauge Railroad.

As the train drew nearer to Silverton, across the valley from us two motorhomes moved slowly along the side of a mountain on what looked like a narrow road high above the Animas River. They maneuvered around a curve and I held my breath for them, hoping they would not slip off the edge of the road and tumble many hundreds of feet below. The road could have been wet from the rainy mist outside. I was glad I was not in their seemingly precarious positions. I was glad, as well, because I didn't know the four of us would be traveling that very same road the next day!

By noon, the train pulled into Silverton for a two-hour layover. First agenda item: lunch.

Walking toward the main street, John spied a restauranteur waving to us to come into Natalia's 1912 Family Restaurant. Drawn by his hospitality, we walked in and were seated at a booth. Soon a woman server took our order and brought our food promptly and graciously. They knew the value of good customer relations and our time frame!

Following lunch, Lib and I meandered through the small town, going in and out of gift shops and an art studio. Paul and John walked around on their own visiting the shops that interested them. Cold mist and snow flurries taunted us. At one point, John caught up with

Lib. He wanted to show her his latest purchase—a good-looking, felt, Western hat.

He went on his way doing other sightseeing and then joined Lib and me at the Grand Imperial Victorian Hotel. A life-sized portrait of Lillian Russell hung in the Victorian lobby. In one of the many gift shops that Paul and John entered, John bought a silver bolo.

Before we knew it, the train whistle blew three times. It was the signal to reboard.

I couldn't resist taking a picture of John wearing his new hat and eating an ice cream cone as he headed back to the train for the return trip.

Before boarding, Paul talked with the brakeman, who stood beside the waiting train. He wanted to know the condition of the train's brakes before the downhill trip to Durango.

Meanwhile, as I neared the train, I noticed that one of the three children who had been on the same train car we were stood by himself on the black metal platform of our train car. Having seen the interaction between the young boy and his siblings and patient par-

"Before boarding, Paul talked with the brakeman, who stood beside the waiting train. He wanted to know the condition of the train's brakes before the downhill trip to Durango."

ents on the way up, I sensed that he was especially challenged in some way. I thought I would help his self-esteem.

"Is this the number 10 car?" I asked.

"Yes, it is," he said.

"Good. That's the one I want," I said.

As I climbed the black metal steps and went past him into the car, thanking him, I heard him say excitedly, "Hey, Mom! I told that old lady the number of our car!"

She must not have heard him the first time. I heard him repeat proudly how he had helped "that old lady."

It was the first time anyone had called me an old lady. Even though my brunette hair has yet to turn gray, there must have been other signs. Or it could simply have been that in a child's mind, all adults are old. Anyway, it made me face the reality of the passing years. The best way to deal with such a comment was, of course, to laugh about it, which Paul, Lib, and John joined in doing when I told them the story.

The return trip took longer than the initial trip because the train had to go slowly and brake often as it chugged mostly downhill. Paul sat beside the window. Riding alongside, I repressed panic at the same scary places we had passed on the way up where the train hung over rock ledges.

One passenger, who had bought a mile-by-mile guide at the Durango train depot, pointed out the place where the Great Train Wreck happened in 1921 near mile marker 471. The train had hit a rock slide, causing the head engine to jump the track and take a second engine with it into the water. One fireman had jumped to safety, but the engineer was injured and another fireman was sadly crushed beneath the wreckage. I looked below toward the river, holding my breath, then smiled when we had safely passed the area. Later I learned that the Durango and Silverton Narrow Gauge Railroad trains carry over 200,000 passengers a year and that the company is very conscientious about using safety measures and doing track and train maintenance to protect passengers.

During the latter part of the ride, for some exercise, Lib and I wobbled back to the refreshment car for a soft drink, dealing with the train's swaying as we went. Each drink was served in a souvenir tall, white, plastic cup with the train's logo and a printed description of the winter holiday excursion on it. While the train normally runs from the end of April to the end of October, it also offers holiday service from the end of November through New Year's Day. From John's comment about souvenir cups in Dodge City, I saved that railroad soda container, not only as a memento but for its potential antique value as well.

It was about six o'clock when the train puffed into the Durango station. As the Graybeals and Paul and I got off, we agreed that we were glad to have taken the trip.

After eating a light supper of sandwiches (since we had had our main meal in Silverton), I did three loads of laundry. I hoped it would be the only time I had to do that chore on the trip. Lib and John had brought along enough clean clothes for the entire trip. Lib said that when she got home, she would wash clothing most of the first day. I planned to follow Lib's idea of taking enough clean clothes for future trips, unless we would be gone more than three weeks.

While I did the laundry, Paul dumped the gray and black water tanks—which he could do at our site at the campground in Durango. He decided to empty the tanks that evening rather than the next morning when we planned to leave. We did not know what facilities might lay ahead the next day as we traveled over mountains and went farther west.

The next day's trip through the San Juan Mountains to Grand Junction should be a short, easy one—only 169 miles. I had been hearing television reports of various mountain passes being closed because of snow and kept an ear open for any mention of a pass closing between Durango and Grand Junction. Surely we would be warned if the road on which we would be traveling was impassable because of snow—we were travelers on Memorial Day weekend. At that time of the year I could not visualize bad weather actually keeping us from going on our merry way.

When Paul finished dumping the tanks, he walked over to the laundry to help carry the clothes that I had folded back to the motorhome. Fifteen minutes later, I completed the task, gathered up the detergent and remaining clothes, and joined Paul. I put away the clean laundry, watched a little television, and went to bed early. Paul stayed up awhile to watch television with the sound off, something that he seemed quite comfortable doing. He often does the same thing at home.

10

Snowbound in the Rockies

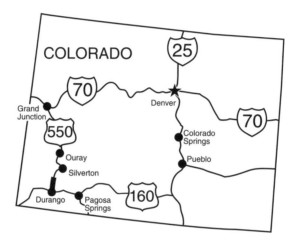

I LISTENED ATTENTIVELY to television reports that Monday morning, the Memorial Day holiday, of the names of certain mountain passes in *northern* Colorado that remained closed due to snow. With no mention of any closed in *southern* Colorado, where we were, I had to assume there were none. In fact, Paul, Lib, John, and I expected to find the famed "Springtime in the Rockies" as we traveled from Durango to Grand Junction, only 169 miles northwest.

Grand Junction was considered the western gateway to Colorado. It had a major airport, provided access to ski areas and summer recreation, and was located among beautiful mesas, red rocks, and green valleys. It lay at an elevation of 4,591 feet and had a population of approximately 29,000. The city of Grand Junction lay in Grand Valley at the junction of the Gunnison and Colorado Rivers.

At 8:50 A.M., we were in our motorhomes with the Graybeals towing their car. We left the campground and headed north on U.S. 550 through the scenic route of the San Juan Mountains, a part of the majestic Rocky Mountains. It was raining.

"This will be a long stretch uphill all the way to the top of the mountain," Paul told me.

In Hermosa, a few miles north of Durango on U.S. 550, John and Lib waited in their Pinnacle on the highway shoulder while Paul filled our motorhome's gasoline tank at a gas station. The friendly woman station attendant said, "The pass is open," and wished us a nice day. Misty rain surrounded us.

With the Graybeals leading, our two coaches and one tow car climbed steadily on the paved, two-lane highway. We moved higher, and the mist became a steady rain.

By 9:32 A.M. we saw snow mixed with rain on the windshield.

As Paul and John talked by CB radio, they anticipated that the snow would be only on our windshields and not accumulate on the road.

"When was the last time you ran into a snowstorm on Memorial Day?" John asked genially.

"I don't think ever," Paul chuckled, confidently.

"I don't think I ever want to again," John said.

"No, I can do without it," Paul responded.

We passed Elbert Creek on our upward trek.

"Snowing to beat the band now," Paul commented to me.

"It does look pretty," I replied, admiring pine branches and mountainsides touched with snow and thanking God silently for the beauty of it all.

We entered San Juan County, crossed Cascade Creek, and continued up the mountain road at 25 miles an hour. I breathed deeply because of scarcer oxygen at that higher altitude.

A sign said "Coal Bank Hill Summit, 4 miles." Paul and I wondered if that was the "pass" to which the gas station attendant referred and if it was at the top of the mountain we were climbing. All around, falling snow continued to create beautiful scenes.

By 9:48 A.M., snow lay on the road. But after a trailer and two cars came from the opposite direction, I reasoned that the mountain road ahead must be passable. Yet our motorhome had begun to move more slowly up the snow-covered road while the Graybeals' moved steadily ahead.

"It's spinning," Paul said as our wheels lost traction and started to spin.

I leaned forward in the passenger seat, hoping my body language would coax the vehicle in its upward climb.

Without fanfare, at 9:53 A.M., Paul took his foot off the accelerator and the motorhome stopped, motionless, in the middle of the right lane, unable to inch ahead. The solid mountain rose on our left, but on our right, beyond a very narrow shoulder with no guardrail, a steep drop-off descended.

Immediately, Paul reached for the CB microphone and called John to tell them we had stopped. John said they would go as far as possible and they continued up the mountain pulling their tow car. Hopefully, John added, if they could reach the summit they would wait for us.

So Coal Bank Hill Summit *was* the top of the mountain. As the Graybeals drove farther away from us and as other people used the same CB channel, we lost voice contact with John and Lib.

We sat still. Fortunately, we had just passed a wide place beside the shoulder of U.S. 550. Paul wanted to back into it to move as far off the road as possible. However, two vans and a car waited directly behind us in the right lane.

"Would you go back there and ask that driver to back up so I can back up?" Paul asked.

Putting on Paul's yellow rain slicker, I tramped outside in falling snow that had become deeper than my white canvas loafers.

A woman driving the first van said, "Ask him to hold on until we turn the vans around. Just hold on!" she repeated anxiously, wanting to avoid any kind of collision.

Hurrying back, I repeated her message to Paul, who had remained in the driver's seat.

At that moment, another woman driving a Class C motorhome (which contains a sleeping or storage area over the cab) came down the mountain toward us. Nearing Paul, she opened her window and asked if she could help. When she applied her brakes, however, her vehicle began to slide toward ours, only about two feet away.

"Keep on going!" Paul shouted quickly to her. "Thank you, anyway," he called after her as she continued down the mountain.

By now, the vans and car behind us had turned and retreated downhill.

Soon another car came up the mountain and stopped behind us. Its driver, a bearded young man in glasses, got out of his car and guided us from outside as Paul slowly backed the motorhome, its wheels sliding, into the snow-covered area adjacent to the road. His good deed done, the young Good Samaritan continued up the mountain.

"We'll have to sit it out, 'cause we sure can't move," Paul announced at 10:09 A.M. The motorhome sat at a rakish angle, pointed uphill, but tilted so that the driver's side was about five inches higher than the passenger's side. The dinette curtains hung away from the windows; my spiral tablet slid off the table when I let go of it. Shakily, I scribbled notes into it. Quiet prevailed for no motors were running. We sat alone inside a leaning, immobile conveyance.

At 10:17 A.M., John called from the summit, where they were parked beside U.S. 550. He said the snow was six inches deep and still coming down and that they would keep the CB turned on.

"Do you think we should dial 911?" I asked Paul, motioning toward our cellular car phone.

Paul considered what to say, then dialed 911. It was 10:20 A.M. The 911 operator referred him to a number for the State Roads Department. A woman at that number could not tell us when a snowplow would open the road to the pass.

Paul then tried to reach Chainsaw, John's CB handle, but could not raise him. We assumed that to conserve chassis battery power, John had turned off their ignition switch, which also turned off their CB. Neither of us had any idea how long we would be at our unexpected roadside "boondock."

(Boondocking, or dry camping, is camping in an RV without the benefit of campground electricity, water, and sewer connections. We had cheerfully boondocked several times during our 44-day tour of Alaska. On that trip, however, such occurrences were planned and the weather was either rainy or dry and warm.)

As if thinking out loud, Paul said that John's tires had only about 17,000 miles of wear on them, whereas ours had about 42,000, satisfactory for wet roads but obviously not for snow. We had steel-belted radial tires with 12-ply sidewalls, otherwise known as all-weather tires. Also, we had a tag axle, whereas John's vehicle did not. That meant John's motorhome had more weight on his drive wheels than we had on ours. The rear weight of our motorhome was spread out over two axles instead of one. Thinking back to an earlier conversation with John on the CB, Paul repeated that John had scarcely made it to the pass. Somebody ahead of him had slipped off to the side and John barely squeezed past.

A minute later, Paul went outside in his yellow slicker to talk with a young man whose van was stuck in the snow toward our left rear. Paul wanted to tell him what he had learned on the telephone about the road. The young man had friends on the Durango-Silverton train whom he was going to meet in Silverton, which was beyond the pass on the other side of the mountain. Several other cars fishtailed up the hill, passing the young man's van and our motorhome, both of which were marooned by the snow.

"He can't go anywhere either," Paul said about the van driver when he came back inside. "Most dangerous thing now is if somebody were to slide into us."

Inside the coach, I paced in the awkwardly tilted aisle, trying to relax, taking deep breaths. I leaned against the dinette table, then sat on the edge of its cushioned seat facing downhill.

I had, of course, heard about people getting caught in unexpected snowstorms and barely escaping with their lives. I wondered what precautions we should have taken. For one, we should have read more about the possible weather changes in high mountain altitudes. For another, we should have bought those new tires. I was so accustomed to living near sea level that I didn't realize the dangers of traveling at higher elevations. I wondered if someone would have to "save" us. It was hard to know what to think or do.

I thought of people who had been stranded *outside* in snow. We at least had the motorhome to protect us from the elements. Yet I was uncertain about when and how we would actually get going again. I tried to remain calm—at least outwardly. Inwardly, I held onto my faith in human ingenuity and that God would provide for us according to our needs. Nevertheless, I continued to feel weak physically and wondered what would happen next.

"Well, they're coming over. Must be clear on the other side," Paul said a little later as vehicles came down the mountain and passed by. One was a tow truck, whose driver stopped and talked with the van driver stuck behind us. To get the latest information, Paul went outside to ask the van driver what he had learned from the tow truck driver.

At the same time, 10:46 A.M., the sheriff of San Juan County drove past without stopping, observing us and the van behind us.

The van driver decided to try getting out of his snowy predicament and, with Paul's help, succeeded in moving his vehicle into the downhill lane. He soon disappeared from view. Paul returned to our coach, his yellow slicker loaded with wet snow. He reported, "The tow truck driver said the snowplow should have been here hours ago. They don't usually let it get like this. The tow truck driver advised, 'If you do get out, I'd go back down the other way.'"

Shortly afterward, Paul hung a thermometer outside to see if we might need to put antifreeze down the kitchen and bath sinks to keep the water valves from freezing. "We might have to stay here all night," he alerted me.

"We just needed a little rest," I said, trying to look on the bright side. "Are we stranded?"

"I would say so," Paul affirmed and added, "But we've got food, we've got warmth, we've got water. I'm glad I dumped the tanks."

"I am, too!"

"I'm certainly not going to try to level," Paul declared, referring to the leveling system with supporting jacks.

"I agree. The jacks would sink down into the mud and freeze tight."

"I don't know about freezing, but they would sink," Paul replied.

Comparing my travel notes in the spiral tablet with a map of the area, I figured that we must be about two miles below the summit. How thankful I was that the roadside area was bordered with boulders and pine trees instead of the steep drop-off where we had stopped originally.

How thankful I was also for the capabilities of the motorhome in our stranded situation. Before we turned the refrigerator/freezer off because it was not level enough to operate properly without damaging it, the refrigerator/freezer had automatically switched its power source to LP gas in order to reserve the coach batteries.

That same LP gas could also supply fuel for the furnace to heat the motorhome and for the hot water heater. I had learned earlier that our LP gas tank holds 21.8 gallons, but we never fill it more than 80 percent. The liquefied gas requires space to vaporize before it leaves the tank. The appliances it serves are designed to use LP gas as vapor. Should LP gas reach an appliance in liquid form, it would be a fire hazard. Our motorhome has an LP gas detector that "sniffs" for LP gas leaks. If one happened, the detector would shut off the LP gas automatically.

We could use the auxiliary generator to run the microwave/convection oven and to supply current for any outlet that needed 120-volt electricity. The generator's source is regular gasoline in the motorhome tank, which we had filled earlier that morning.

We also had the coach and chassis batteries. The *coach* batteries supplied 12 volts of direct current to energize the interior lights and water pump that sent water to the faucets, shower, and toilet. The *chassis* batteries supplied voltage and current to start the engine and operate accessories such as the lights, dash instruments, windshield wipers, cruise control, dash air, radio, automatic electric steps, and refrigerator/freezer. If the chassis batteries became low in our stranded situation, we were in trouble.

Another van, with a Texas license plate, crept slowly past us going uphill and stopped just ahead, unable to advance. It was 10:59 A.M. As I watched, a woman got out and took a picture. That reminded me—I donned the yellow slicker and went outside. I used my hand to shield my camera from the falling snow and then snapped images of our plight in Colorado's Rocky Mountains in the "spring-time" on Memorial Day.

When I was back inside, Paul announced that the temperature was 34 degrees at 11:02 A.M. He and I were sitting lopsided on the uphill side of the coach, he on the sofa and I perched on the dinette seat. Two women from the Texas van in front of us knocked on our door and asked if they might use our bathroom.

We welcomed them and soon began exchanging travel stories. As we talked, the husband of the younger woman came to the door to let them know that the snowplow had gone past. He wanted to try getting out. The women thanked us and the man offered to help us get our motorhome out, but Paul decided the task was too big for the two of them. Subsequently, the Texan driver worked his van out onto the road and vanished up the mountain, leaving us alone again.

"There goes the sheriff," Paul said as the marked car, on a return trip, went past us up the hill, again without stopping.

"Well, the snowplow might have gone, but it hasn't done me any good," Paul said, carefully examining the road through the window.

"What will we need to do to get out of here?" I asked.

"I'm not sure yet. When it stops snowing, I'm going to do more looking. It is getting brighter outside," he observed at 11:37 A.M.

Hope flowed into my apprehension.

"I need either cinders or a bare road. Right now, as soon as I put the power to it, it'll spin," Paul said of the motorhome a couple of minutes later. "I can see the middle line on the road—must be getting a little softer." Spreading cinders on the snowy area would have helped to give the wheels traction, but of course, we didn't have any on board.

"Snow does seem to be slowing a little," I replied, squinting out the windows to be sure.

"Starting to get a little slushy," Paul observed. "I think I'll go out and clean the windshield off." He got the long-handled broom from under the sofa and once more put on his slicker, adding gloves.

"Yeah, John and Libby will be okay sitting up there on that summit," Paul assured us both as he stepped outside.

Alone and on the verge of shakiness again, I took more deep breaths in that high altitude.

At 11:45 A.M., almost two hours after we had lost traction on snow-covered U.S. 550, the snowfall thinned out and all but stopped. Traffic continued passing both ways, up and down the hill.

After cleaning the windshield of its white blanket, Paul joined me in eating a few small pretzels. We had turned off the refrigerator when backing into that lopsided spot and did not want to open the door unnecessarily. Since we also wanted to conserve our propane gas, the furnace was turned off. To keep warm, I wore Paul's warm, blue, fleecy jacket and my own fleece-lined, zippered boots.

Restless, Paul went back outside. It had been only fifteen minutes since the snow stopped and already the temperature had shot up to 42 degrees. Happily, Paul discovered cinders instead of mud beneath the snow and, using the broom, he cleared two tracks for backing the motorhome onto the road.

Soon he re-entered the motorhome and sat behind the steering wheel.

"You go outside and watch to be sure I stay in those cleared tracks," Paul directed me.

Already dressed for outdoors, I quickly donned a clear plastic rain scarf and trooped outside. I saw two narrow paths extending behind the motorhome toward the highway. With high hopes, I watched Paul carefully back the motorhome away from its emergency roadside haven onto the road. He followed his cleared tracks as if he were a train engineer. Fearful that other vehicles would come up the mountain while we paused in the right lane, I hurried back inside and into the passenger seat, hastily snapping together the seat belt.

Paul slowly pressed down on the accelerator, the motor revved, and the motorhome moved forward. I held my breath for fear we would not keep going.

"Hang on, it may not be this good farther up," Paul cautioned as he peered intensely ahead, hands grasping the steering wheel. "I've got the power if I can just get the traction."

Sitting upright, I scrawled in my spiral tablet, "11:59 A.M. Got out and gunning. Praying again."

I saw melting slush on the road in our lane that allowed hard pavement to show. As we continued determinedly toward the summit, Paul needed both hands for driving. He told me to get on the CB and see if I could raise John and Lib.

"Chainsaw, can you hear me? This is Reindeer." No response.

"Chainsaw, can you hear? This is Reindeer. Chainsaw, this is Reindeer. Can you hear me?" I repeated.

"They must have their CB turned off," Paul concluded.

Breathless from altitude and anxiety, I focused on the inclined road ahead, holding my seat, hoping we could keep moving. We did not know how far ahead the pass was. At least it was not snowing.

"There they are!" I shouted. Ahead, at the summit, I saw the familiar cream and green Pinnacle parked beside the road. It was 12:06 P.M. when Paul blew our horn as we passed them and I waved joyfully to Lib and John sitting at their dinette table eating lunch. John came on the CB. He said they had had their CB off. We had turned ours off for a while also.

*"'There they are!' I shouted. . . . At the summit [Coal Bank Pass Summit],
I saw the familiar cream and green Pinnacle parked beside the road."*

Paul pulled into the parking area just beyond them. A large sign stood boldly nearby: "Coal Bank Pass Summit, Elev 10,640 ft." I took a deep breath. We had reached the pass.

Paul let the motor run as he went outside to talk with the Graybeals. They agreed that if the road was not bare of snow, they would not try going down the other side until it was. Since the temperature was warmer and the snow had stopped, they thought it was safe to descend.

Meanwhile, I took pictures and occasionally stood still to experience the summit. I breathed in deeply the pure mountain air and gazed in wonderment at snow-covered peaks and snow-laden evergreens, both nearby and far, far away. In addition to the magnificent vistas, I admired the hardy souls who had first pioneered that route.

Now that we were on top, the pass seemed like a simple idea, just a place where some earlier travelers found it possible to get over the mountain. I hoped they did not have to travel over it in winter.

The highest pass in Colorado, Trail Ridge Road Pass, reaches 12,183 feet in northern Colorado. The lowest, Douglas Pass, measures 8,268 feet in the north-central area. Between these two extremes lies

Coal Bank Hill Pass, in southwestern Colorado, at 10,640 feet, which was part of our route on that Memorial Day.

As for myself, a modern pioneer who enjoys the comforts of our home away from home, I would revere those awesome Rocky Mountains in Colorado with their unpredictable, stranding snow—snow to be reckoned with and yet beautiful snow, snow that would surely help nourish the blooms of spring as it melted into precious water. Perhaps that day we did see—in its earliest stage—"springtime in the Rockies."

Paul returned from talking with the Graybeals.

"I'm going to pull off farther so John can go ahead. He has better traction and I don't want to hold him up."

Then John said over the CB, "Paul, you'd better go ahead. I can't see well enough to go ahead." Our motorhome was blocking his view of oncoming traffic.

My brother-in-law, Al Guyer, has a favorite question that he asks of people who have gone through a difficult situation: And what did you learn from that? Well, I could answer, I learned that one should expect any kind of weather in higher altitudes and that it's best to be prepared for the worst. I also learned from Paul the patience of working *with* the weather, whatever it turns out to be.

And with that thought in mind and future lessons to be learned, we prepared to descend from the summit of Coal Bank Hill in our quest toward Grand Junction, Colorado.

11

Million Dollar Highway

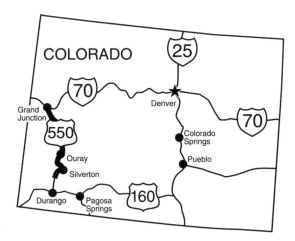

TWO MORE MOUNTAIN SUMMITS and the towns of Silverton, Ouray, Montrose, and Delta lay between Coal Bank Hill Pass, where our caravan stood poised to descend, and our goal for the day, Grand Junction, Colorado. We had spent that Memorial Day morning covering about 29 miles of the 169-mile trip.

Between Durango and Silverton rose Coal Bank Hill Summit at 10,640 feet and Molas Pass at 10,910 feet; between Silverton and Grand Junction rose the even higher Red Mountain Pass at 11,008 feet.

Paul and I had not eaten lunch but thought only briefly about that as we pulled away from the snow-laden Coal Bank Hill Pass at 12:14 P.M. With the Graybeals behind us towing their car, we headed downhill toward Silverton, the same town that we had explored the day before via the narrow gauge railroad train.

Anyone who has traveled on mountain roads knows that they do not go directly up a mountain, over the top, and directly down again on the other side. Instead, mountain roads can briefly go straight ahead; curve sharply; switch back and forth from one curve to another; rise high above valleys, canyons, and gorges; incline or decline steeply; hug the mountain on one side and hover over a drop-off on the other—all the while ascending or descending in elevation over or around the mountain.

Some mountain roads are paved four-lane highways with an extra passing lane on uphill stretches. Others are paved two-lane roads with no passing allowed at unsafe places. Some less-traveled roads remain unpaved. Mountain roads with long, steep declines sometimes offer pull-off ramps for trucks and other runaway vehicles when their brakes fail. Like roller coasters, merry-go-rounds, and Ferris wheels, mountain roads can entertain and thrill even though they are meant to be safe.

I have discovered that riding in the passenger seat of a motorhome, which is much higher than in an automobile, gives one a great panoramic view. But when I look down the side of the motorhome toward the ground, I can't see the wheels or how close they are to the shoulder of the road or the edge of a long drop-off. That optical illusion often makes me think our motorhome is too close to the edge of the road and increases my sense of danger. When that happens, I remind myself of that phenomenon and that Paul is a steady, careful driver. Yet there are some times and some roads where the optical illusion is just too overpowering.

U.S. 550 from Durango to Grand Junction was a paved, two-lane road. Little dots on our map showed it as a "scenic route" from Durango to Ouray. So far, that certainly was true.

At 12:14 P.M., both our motorhomes left the side of the road at Coal Bank Hill Pass, heading toward Molas Pass and then Silverton. We all expected that the worst was over, not knowing that ahead was an even more harrowing descent down the other side of the unfamiliar San Juan Mountain.

"I'm going to put it in low going down here," Paul said to John on the CB.

"Okay, that's what I've got," John replied.

As we went downhill, on my right was a long drop-off without guardrails! A big snowplow came toward us. I held my breath as it passed us successfully.

Ahead I saw a curve with a guardrail. I leaned in toward the center of the motorhome, hoping my body language would help to keep the motorhome from going over the edge of the road. Beyond the curve ahead I couldn't see anything but sky.

The mountain was on Paul's side, the gorge on my side. Paul put on the brakes to let traffic pass. I gritted my teeth as a big 18-wheeler truck thundered past us.

We negotiated the curve and Paul said on the CB to John, "I kinda wish you would go ahead of us." He pulled gingerly to the side of the road and the Graybeals passed us.

Shortly, a sign announced "Molas Pass Summit, 4 miles."

"It's nice to do Colorado in winter, spring, and summer all in one vacation," John said on the CB.

"Yeah, as long as one of those doesn't trip you up somewhere," Paul answered back.

I got up from the passenger seat and wobbled back to turn on the refrigerator now that the motorhome was back on the highway in a level position rather than tilted.

Paul shifted into the lowest gear as the motorhome climbed once again, this time toward Molas Pass. When no drop-offs intrigued or frightened me, I admired the beauty of snow on pine trees.

"I think it's stopped snowing," I said.

"I hope so. I was surprised that the temperature jumped from 34 to 42 in that short a time."

We continued climbing uphill with the Graybeals well ahead.

Then John came on the CB, "Up here at the top, 10,910." He had reached Molas Pass Summit and we soon followed suit.

A few seconds later we began descending. John and Paul slowly and carefully passed another snowplow coming toward us. "Pretty much just wet," Paul said of the bare road ahead. Everywhere else, snow covered the landscape.

"Chainsaw, there's no way I would have started down this side this morning until the roads were clear," Paul said over the CB.

"Definitely not!" John agreed.

We continued down a steep grade. "Slide Area," a sign warned. The highway continued to be two lanes with snow on the shoulders, a drop-off on my right, and no guardrails.

The day before as we rode the narrow gauge railroad train from Durango to Silverton, from across a wide valley I had seen motorhomes the size of ours creeping along a road high above the level of the train. They looked like they were on a narrow ledge above a rocky precipice. As the train moved along, I could barely watch for it looked like they might slip off the road and tumble down the mountain at any moment. My heart leaped into my throat for them. Today, we were on that same road. I hardly dared breathe or move except to lean in the direction of safety.

"There's Silverton!" Paul said as we came into view of the valley and village. I saw the Durango-Silverton train track far, far below to my right across the wide valley where we had been the day before. Ahead, the distant town and the tiny tracks leading to it looked like a historic village suddenly appearing from nowhere, like Never-Never Land in *Peter Pan* or the mythical land in *Camelot*.

"A small rock just went across the road," Paul said. That rock, the size of a grapefruit, made rock slides realistic for me. Before that, I thought that they were extremely rare occurrences and that they happened only to other people.

Worrying about the rock slide possibility and the high, narrow, curving road on which we drove, I could barely look ahead at Silverton.

"This is worse than Skagway. It was straighter," said Paul, referring to the highway that we had driven over that went from Whitehorse, Yukon Territory, into Skagway, Alaska.

"'There's Silverton!' Paul said as we came into view of the valley and village. I saw the Durango-Silverton train track far, far below to my right across the wide valley where we had been the day before. Ahead, the distant town and the tiny tracks leading to it looked like a historic village suddenly appearing from nowhere, like Never-Never Land in Peter Pan *or the mythical land in* Camelot.*"*

"We didn't have these weather and road conditions either," I added.

I said farewell to the distant town of Silverton, thinking that we would soon bypass it. But when we were almost down the hill, John suggested that we stop at a large gravel area where the snow had melted so that Paul and I could eat lunch. It was 12:50 P.M.

The Graybeals kindly waited while we ate a quick lunch. During lunch, even unflappable Paul said he felt weak after his driving experience that morning.

While we ate, John walked around taking pictures. After lunch, I took a photo of Silverton, which lay ahead and to our right, stepping carefully to find hard places in the wet, muddy gravel. Although in a valley, Silverton claimed an elevation of 9,318 feet.

Paul stepped outside, as he often did when we parked, to look for obvious problems by checking the tires and looking for signs of any fluid leaks.

Before he got into the driver's seat again, I looked in one of our travel guides to see what lay ahead. It told of a six-mile stretch of U.S. 550 between Silverton and Ouray named the Million Dollar Highway that had steep cliffs and steep drop-offs. The guide recommended that travelers using it drive cautiously. I was uncertain as to the meaning of the highway's name. I thought it could apply to the cost of reconstructing the road, to the value of the ore from local mines, or to spectacular views. It ranked high in the nation as a breathtaking automobile route.

Having just come through a perilous stretch of U.S. 550, having driven on the Top of the World Highway in Yukon Territory and Alaska, and having traveled from Whitehorse to Skagway, I questioned whether the Million Dollar Highway would be any more hazardous than those infamous roads.

After lunch, our two-family caravan continued descending the mountain on U.S. 550, passing a road on the right leading into Silverton. My throat felt dry and my ears popped when I swallowed.

"Wonder how long we stopped back there this morning," Paul said, referring to our involuntary snowy boondock.

I looked at my spiral tablet notes and figured. "Two hours and six minutes. I have: '9:53 Stopped,' and '11:59 Got out and gunning.' That's two hours and six minutes."

Paul laughed out loud and repeated, "Got out and gunning."

U.S. 550 to Grand Junction continued to hold our interest. A sign said "No Stopping Next 1³/₄ miles." Another read "Red Mountain Summit, 5 miles." We were on the Million Dollar Highway section of U.S. 550.

Deeply snow-covered mountains were all around as we negotiated a sharp switchback and continued uphill. Again there were no guardrails and the steep drop-off was on my side of the road.

"They just carved the road out of the side of the hill. What they had left they pushed over the side after they made the road flat enough," Paul observed.

I opened my mouth and held it wide open as the shoulder on my side narrowed to barely 10 inches. That stretch of U.S. 550 was a two-lane, paved road with a double yellow stripe in the middle and a white line along the edge.

"The white line almost missed the road there," Paul said of another place where there was *no* road shoulder, just the edge of a sheer cliff.

I can't look, I said to myself and held my head down with my hands after I saw the steep drop-off on my side. No wonder the sign said No Stopping. Where would one stop but in the middle of the traffic lane?

We entered Ouray County.

"Look over there, dear. Isn't that pretty?" Paul said. I could barely look but I managed to see what he saw—the sun shining on a snow-topped mountain in the distance.

"Avalanche Area, Icy Road," Paul read a sign and added, "Well, I'd rather hope it won't be."

I had not eaten the crispy rice bar still lying in its wrapper on the hump beside my seat where I had placed it earlier. It was to be dessert for lunch.

The Graybeals waved to us as we maneuvered a switchback.

"Whoa! Whoa! Paul! I think you're going too fast," came out of my lips. With my hands cupped over closed eyes, I lowered my head and bent toward his seat. It was the first time I had ever told him that.

Paul chuckled and continued talking with John on the CB. They wondered why the engineers had not made the Million Dollar Highway wider.

At the next opportunity, Paul pulled over into a gravel area to let cars pass us going downhill. More switchbacks were ahead, according to a sign.

As we continued downhill, Paul said, "Look up there. Isn't that beautiful?"

"It is. It is indeed," I managed. I saw high mountains, snow-covered and brilliantly white. But at that moment, I thought that nothing on our trip would compare with the excitement of the drive that day.

We reached the valley and I took a deep breath of relief. That was the scariest ride I had *ever* been on.

"Red Mountain Creek," Paul read a sign out loud.

I swiveled out of my passenger seat and got a drink of water for my dry throat.

My relief was short-lived as we went downhill again. At mile marker 88 a sign said "Snowshed Ahead." We passed stones lying in the road. High above the canyon on a road without guardrails, we crept along. The drop-off this time was on Paul's side and the jagged rocks on mine. Brave as I was, the drive made me close my eyes, hold my breath, and think if I ever got down safely, I'd never come that way again!

"Pretty waterfall on the left," Paul said. Still closing my eyes, I visualized what Paul was describing. No words could get me to look at anything other than the insides of my eyelids.

"Tunnel," Paul announced as we went through a short one. My ears needed to pop as I swallowed. I opened my eyes in the brief respite of the tunnel.

Paul chuckled. "When it said 15 miles per hour, it means 15 miles per hour," he said, referring to a speed limit sign.

"I tell you we couldn't have hit a prettier day to come through here once we got on this side of Coal Bank Hill Pass," Paul said at 2:01 P.M. I had no comment.

Downward we continued.

Around a curve, a sign announced "Switzerland America Lookout Point." A village below looked like a picturesque Swiss town with the Alps all around. Ouray was the town. We were at the end of the Million Dollar Highway. We descended switchbacks into the midst of quaint, interesting houses and shops. Both of my ears were "temporarily closed" due to the uneven atmospheric pressure caused by descending from the high altitude of the mountains.

Named for the Ute chieftain, Ouray is a tourist town with a normal population of 600. Even though we had descended from a mountain to reach the town, Ouray's elevation was still a high 7,710 feet. Its architectural charm, million-gallon natural hot springs pool, and outdoor activities, such as skiing, Jeep tours, and camping, draw visitors year-round. We drove slowly through the main street, admiring its chalets and colorful stores.

Passing through Ouray on U.S. 550, we continued toward Grand Junction. We were in a ranching and farming valley going downhill gradually.

"Llama on the left," John said by CB. We looked in time to see several of these wooly, long-necked animals walking and grazing in a meadow. Immigrants from South America, these animals could be used as beasts of burden or shorn for their fleece, which could be woven into wool cloth. Somehow we didn't expect to see them in Colorado.

Since his feet were getting hot, Paul changed from fleece-lined boots to slippers as he drove the motorhome. I assisted by getting the slippers from the motorhome wardrobe closet and helping him remove the boots, all while he sat behind the steering wheel. (At home, however, Paul normally gets his own slippers and removes his own boots!)

"We're just riding along the edge of a valley," Paul said.

"This is a nice relief after the wild ride," I commented.

We entered Montrose County and drove through a road construction area, which was a picnic after the treacherous roads earlier that day. We passed two medium-sized feed yards in the long valley.

A roadside sign said "Montrose, Elevation 5,794 feet." We drove through its wide main street and continued toward Grand Junction, 61 miles ahead. My right ear opened, but noises to my left still sounded distant.

"Buffalo on the left," John told us as we traveled once again in open country. A buffalo herd grazed in a large fenced area.

Signs announced "Delta County," then "Delta, 4,961 feet elevation." After we had traveled through Delta, I jotted in my spiral tablet:

> My left ear opened. We are driving in a wide, wide valley with buttes, mesas, and mountains on the right and

rolling hills on the left. Semi-arid, desert brush. No fences. Open range.

We entered Mesa County. Evergreen bushes grew randomly on the range land along with other desert flora. On my right, about 10 ostriches walked or stood with a high-and-mighty countenance in a small fenced yard adjacent to low wood sheds. We seemed to be driving through a zoo of unexpected creatures!

Just before we reached the outskirts of Grand Junction, we saw great buttes and mesas on the right in a long line. Their stratified (layered) soil looked sandy, brown, and shadowy.

At 4:11 P.M., Paul and John drove into the Big J RV Park at Grand Junction, Colorado. I waited in the passenger seat for Paul to register at the office. Oh, mercy, I thought, the day's events in the snowstorm and perilous roads vivid in my memory and emotions. Mercy, mercy, mercy! How grateful I was that we survived!

The manager of Big J RV Park called a nearby restaurant that he liked to make sure it was open on the holiday. After finding our campsites and hooking up the motorhomes to electricity and water, John unhitched the tow car. Soon Lib, John, Paul, and I sat at a booth table by a window in Bob and Jan's Prime Rib & Lobster House.

John said even he felt weak from the harrowing drive. On the way up Coal Bank Hill after we had been stranded, snow clung to his windshield, so he had to lean to the right to see clearly. That meant making constant adjustments of the motorhome's position on the road. At one point, he had had to take the inside lane to pass a stalled car in the right lane.

Even after that emotionally exhausting day, Lib looked radiant with her short, chic, platinum hair and wearing a light gray sweater and gray pants. Smiling, she said the downhill part was just as bad as the uphill. She was not sure she ever wanted to go to Colorado again. I knew I never wanted to travel *that* road again, unless it were wider and had good guardrails.

Exhausted, we all sat there, glad to *be* there—one of the times when life was very real and we were so thankful to be a part of it. When John's and Lib's salads and Paul's and my soups came, I asked if we could have a special prayer of thanksgiving. All agreed and bowed their heads. Paul prayed aloud, thanking God for safe travel, our good time together, and the food we were about to eat—an earnest prayer.

Over dinner, we recounted the day's adventures. Since Paul had chuckled about it, I read to Lib and John the brief entries from my spiral tablet: "9:53 A.M. Stopped." "11:59 A.M. Got out and gunning. Praying again." There were laughs all around.

In the high altitude, I continued to struggle with weakness, conscious breathing, tiredness, shakiness, and slight dizziness at times, so I didn't offer much conversation, but I listened and enjoyed taking in the reactions and stories of the others.

We lingered over the meal. John ate a chocolate sundae for dessert while I finished a London broil with mushroom gravy. As usual, Lib refused dessert as did Paul. We relaxed and eventually the conversation turned away from the day's events to topics such as how humor relates to intelligence.

After dinner, as we left the restaurant John said he would like a copy of my trip notes, that I could just print an extra copy for him when I printed mine. I happily agreed to do so.

Back at the campground, wanting a little dessert and answers to some questions, I walked from our campsite a short distance over to the office and store. Don O'Brien, the manager, told me they usually had 89-degree weather by Memorial Day, but that year he had not even been able to paint the inside of his swimming pool—a task that required 70-degree temperatures—so he did not have his heated pool ready.

Don said our drive that day over the passes was the most beautiful one in *summer*, but in other seasons he sent people *around* the passes! *Now* we knew! But then again, I wondered whether we would have taken the alternate route even if someone had told us about it. I'm sure it would have depended on the source of the information and whether we understood just how dangerous the mountain roads could be.

Personable, articulate, and service-oriented, Don O'Brien stood out among RV park owners. He said Big J was the nickname for Grand Junction, thus the name of the Big J RV Park. I bought postcards and an ice cream popsicle before leaving the camp store.

It had taken us all day to travel the 169 miles from Durango, a trip that would have taken only three hours on an interstate at 55 miles per hour. But we had safely reached our destination on that Memorial Day holiday, a day we would not soon forget.

How glad I was for our cautious, competent drivers. I wondered how they would be tested the next day as we moved from Grand Junction northeast over mountains to Denver.

When we travel in the motorhome with all of its conveniences, it is *home* to us. After a day of sightseeing, travel, or high adventure like we encountered that Memorial Day, we're glad to relax in its cozy, familiar comforts, watching television and reminiscing.

12

Glenwood Hot Springs

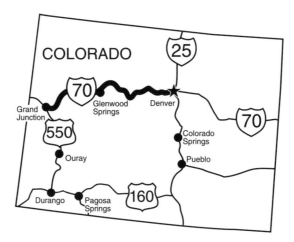

THE TOPOGRAPHY OF COLORADO is roughly divided from east to west into thirds. The eastern third contains great plains of relatively flat land and cities such as Fort Collins, Boulder, Denver, Colorado Springs, and Pueblo (where we camped when we first entered Colorado). The middle third features the Rocky Mountains, which contain the Front Range with Pikes Peak, the Sangre de Cristo Mountains, the Park Range, the Sawatch Range, and the San Juan Mountains (through which we drove to reach Grand Junction). The western third contains the Colorado Plateau with its valleys, deep canyons, and mesas.

It was through the Colorado Plateau and the Rocky Mountains that we headed on Tuesday, May 30, northeast from Grand Junction toward the west side of Denver, Colorado. With Monday's hair-raising experience still fresh in my memory, I forced myself to be optimistic about the safety of the coming day's travel. Our motorhome drivers had been heroic in the way they handled both the vehicles and themselves on the precipitous roads the day before.

During the night it rained and it remained overcast at 7:30 on that Tuesday morning. Paul walked to the campground office for a newspaper.

When he returned, he said that John wanted to buy propane before we left the campground. Many campgrounds offer LP gas service. Campers simply drive their motorhomes to the campground's large tank, where a campground employee puts the LP gas into the motorhome propane gas tank.

Paul and I sat across the dinette table from one another sharing the newspaper. We were ready to leave the campground when John finished his coffee and bought propane. We both wore swim suits under our clothes, prepared for a visit to Glenwood Hot Springs Pool later that morning.

"Seems like the whole state of Colorado has had crazy weather this year, the way people here talk," Paul commented. Don at the office had told Paul that Grand Junction had had rain every night for weeks, which was highly unusual.

I felt slightly nauseated and short of breath. I knew that I should continue to pace myself in the high altitude. I didn't have the tense, tight feeling in my chest and arms of the previous day, but then that day's travel had delivered one exciting thrill after another.

Just before nine o'clock, we left the Big J RV Park at Grand Junction, our farthest point west in Colorado, and headed northeast to Glenwood Springs, en route to Denver.

At Clifton, just a few miles outside of Grand Junction, we filled our rigs with gasoline and calculated our gas mileage. John got 7.9 miles per gallon and we 6.7 over the passes from Durango to Grand Junction.

"Biggest thing was we just got through," John said over the CB about our drive through the mountains the day before.

"You're right. I wouldn't have cared if it were *two* miles to the gallon," replied Paul.

We were on I-70 going east to Glenwood Springs and had the opportunity to take scenic Route 65.

"I think we'll pass on the scenic highway," John in the lead said on the CB.

"Yes," Paul concurred. "I think we've had enough scenic highways for a day or two."

"It might even last into Friday or Saturday," John said.

Actually, I-70 itself was designated a scenic route on our map. At the moment, the Colorado River flowed alongside in a canyon.

"Now this is the kind of highway I like," I said. The dual highway had guardrails and a center concrete barrier.

"Ho! Ho! No challenge or thrill with this," Paul teased.

"Okay with me."

It continued to rain. While the main advantage of traveling in May was that we didn't have to share the road or campgrounds with summer tourists, the disadvantage entailed uncertain weather—rain and snow.

My nose dripped and my throat felt sore that morning. If we indulged ourselves in the hot water at Glenwood Springs, I hoped it would miraculously cure my beginning cold.

At the city of Glenwood Springs, we drove around awhile before finding a place to park our small caravan. We walked a short distance to the Hot Springs Lodge and Pool. It was 11:36 A.M.

The hot springs were part of a modern complex that included a bathhouse, sport shop, restaurant/lounge, athletic club, and 107-unit lodge. The lodge uses the hot springs for heating and is the largest building to be heated geothermally in Colorado.

Inside the Hot Springs Lodge and Pool, we bought passes for the pool, then found the men's and women's changing rooms. Lib and I put our street clothes in lockers provided there. Barefooted and wearing only our swim suits, Lib and I walked toward the two outdoor pools, giggling and shivering in the cold, rainy weather.

As the world's largest natural hot springs pool, the main pool is 405 feet long and 100 feet wide. It contains 1,071,000 gallons of water at a temperature of 90 degrees. The adjacent small pool is 100 feet long. It contains 91,000 gallons at a temperature of 104 degrees. The water temperature when it comes from the springs is approximately 124 degrees. The springs produce a daily inpouring of 3,500,000 gallons of water. Two 40-horsepower pumps push the water through filters at the rate of 3,800 gallons per minute. The water in the large pool is changed every six hours and in the small pool every two hours.

Lib and I walked to the edge of the large pool. We soon joined John and Paul and others floating and splashing around in the soothing mineral water. With steam rising around us, we discovered that the warmest places were at the openings midway across and on the bottom of the pool where fresh hot water flowed in. Later we ventured into the smaller, warmer pool.

"The hot springs [Glenwood Springs] were part of a modern complex that included a bathhouse, sport shop, restaurant/lounge, athletic club, and 107-unit lodge. . . . Barefooted and wearing only our swim suits, Lib and I walked toward the two outdoor pools, giggling and shivering in the cold, rainy weather . . . . We soon joined John and Paul and others floating and splashing around in the soothing mineral water."

Paul found a series of chairs near the opposite wall in the larger pool. For 25 cents, a machine almost immersed him in bubbling vibrations of warm water for five minutes.

"Hey! This is great! I could stay in here all day!" he shouted to us, smiling and playful as a child. He ended up spending 75 cents.

During a relaxing lunch in the adjacent Glenwood Hot Springs Restaurant, we watched other people enjoying the hot springs through the restaurant windows. After lunch, we walked back to our motorhomes under cloudy skies and damp, cold air. It was 1:46 P.M. when we continued in our coaches toward Denver. The rain had stopped momentarily while we were in the hot springs, but we ran into sporadic showers as we drove.

From Glenwood Springs we regained I-70 east and entered a 12-mile-long segment of highway through Glenwood Canyon that took 17 years to construct at a cost of $480 million. Engineers not only designed the highway to preserve the natural beauty of the canyon but also provided for a number of rest areas for RVers and others to enjoy the views. Along the river side of the road ran a concrete path for bikers, hikers, and others to travel safely away from vehicle traffic. Fishing was available at several of the rest areas.

Colorado's skiing is reputed to be the best in the world; most of the state's ski resorts have powderlike snow and terrain for skiers from beginners through advanced to "extreme." Lodging also is varied, ranging from bed and breakfasts to full-service hotels. Paul and I have friends who fly to Colorado to ski. Neither the Graybeals nor Paul and I skied; however, I wanted to see what a Colorado ski resort looked like.

Over the CB, we decided not to take exit 176 to Vail but to see whatever we could from I-70 as we passed that resort town. With a population of about 4,000 and an elevation of about 8,150 feet, Vail was designed to resemble an Alpine ski village. As the largest single-mountain ski resort in North America, it offers both winter sports and summer activities, such as hiking and mountain biking.

Soon great masses of modern lodges and individual high-priced homes appeared on both sides of I-70. They sat placidly in the valley below numerous ski slopes. No skiers that day schussed down the slopes—the snow had melted on the lower areas of the mountainsides and bare ground was obvious. That was the sum total of my encounter with Vail skiing.

In the high altitude, I was content to ride along, look at sights, and jot down notes. I had no energy for listening to the Christian Writers Conference tapes that were at my feet or using the laptop computer.

We climbed toward Vail Pass. John had his four-way flashers on.

"I have mine on, too," Paul said to me.

The bicycle path running parallel to the highway on my side of the motorhome was clear, but it had snow banks four or five feet deep on both sides. At 3:25 P.M. we reached Vail Pass Summit, elevation 10,603 feet.

"All downhill from here," Paul said as we continued toward Denver. He changed his mind 20 minutes later as we climbed again, high above a narrow valley. "I said back there a ways it was all down-hill, but I don't believe it is," he said.

As we ascended the hill, we encountered more snow with fog. The wipers swooshed at normal speed, the Graybeals' and our flashers blinked from the slow lane.

"As long as she melts, I don't mind," Paul commented, referring to the snow.

We passed a truck in the slow lane and I waved to the driver. He gave me a nice smile and waved back.

"That's nice that you waved to him. Friendly and good PR for RVs," said Paul.

We reached the Eisenhower Memorial Tunnel, elevation 11,013 feet, at the summit of Straight Creek Pass. In the long tunnel, the highway looked and felt like it was going downhill, but I thought that might be an optical illusion. Leaving the tunnel, we indeed contin-ued downhill at a fairly steep grade in fog and mist. Fine snow began falling, and the temperature was close to 25 degrees.

"I never thought Colorado was going to be this exciting," I remarked.

"Well, because they [John and Lib] talked about the time of year they did, I'm not surprised at any of this," Paul said, referring to his thoughts that the weather in late spring might be unpredictably intemperate.

"Colorado has a lot to offer visitors," I observed, thinking of its breathtaking scenery; historic sites; Native American arts and crafts; Western milieu of ranches; friendly people; wide, open ranges; big fields and sky; and modern city of Denver with its museums and new airport.

"Our exit coming up," John beamed over the CB.

"Okay," Paul answered.

Soon we drove into Prospect RV Park & Campground in Wheat Ridge, a suburb west of Denver, and stopped at the office as usual.

While Paul made sure he had everything he needed before leaving the driver's seat, John walked to our driver's door window. Paul slid it open.

"What do you think? Four or five nights?" John asked Paul.

"Whatever you think is fine with me," Paul replied.

The fellows registered at the nearby office for only one night because the registrar was too busy to do the paperwork for more nights. The campground was crowded.

Paul backed the motorhome into our campsite then went outside in the rain to hook up to water and electricity. It was 5:30 P.M. and we had reached our goal for that day without mishap. I was thankful to the engineers who had designed I-70 between Grand Junction and Denver, not only for the excellent multilaned highway itself but for the way they preserved the beauty of the drive.

After supper in the motorhome, I took a nap on the sofa and then went to bed. My nose had been dripping all day. The hot springs didn't cure my cold symptoms. Paul had the living room area to himself as he read a newspaper and then watched television with the sound muted. Apparently the high altitude was not bothering him.

The next day, Wednesday, we planned to leave at a leisurely 10:00 in the tow car to find a shoe repair shop for Paul and a mall salon for my hairdo.

At some point during our visit to Denver, we hoped to ride several miles south to visit Paul's sister Hazel and her husband, Al Guyer. Although they were actually residents of Pennsylvania, they were camp co-managers for a Church of the Brethren outdoor facility called Camp Colorado during that summer. I wanted to be well enough in case we could arrange that side trip. Hazel had not been enthusiastic about spending that summer at Camp Colorado but consented to do so because it was something Al felt God called him to do.

There were so many things to see and do in Denver that we hardly knew what to choose. Attractions we considered included the Denver Zoo, the Denver Museum of Natural History, the Colorado History Museum, the Denver Art Museum, the Molly Brown House Museum, the state capitol, and the United States Mint. We wished we had time to see them all.

13

Camp Colorado

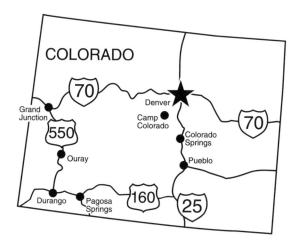

AT FOUR O'CLOCK the next morning, Wednesday, May 31, I got out of my motorhome bed, took a pain reliever caplet for my stuffy headache, and gargled with salt water to alleviate my scratchy throat. Even at that hour, I thought of wanting to be well enough for a visit to Camp Colorado, which I hoped we would be able to fit into our sightseeing time while in the Denver area.

Before sleep came again, my mind played with titles for my first motorhome book: So You Think You Want a Motorhome, Miles of Smiles by Motorhome.

Later that morning, John and Paul registered at the office for four more nights.

The sun shone as the four of us piled into the tow car and headed out of the campground on errands and for sightseeing. First, Lib, John, and I waited in the car while Paul carried his leather shoes to the shoe repair shop. I spied a drugstore next door. I wondered out loud if it might offer something specific for my cold symptoms. Lib encouraged me to go in.

The pharmacist inside recommended nonprescription cold therapy tablets. He kindly provided a paper cup with water for me to take the first tablet. I was very grateful. I wanted to halt the cold early.

Driving on, by this time in rain, we found the Westminster Mall in Denver. Lib had her nails manicured in another salon while a stylist at Regis Hair Salon shampooed and blow-dried my hair. Meanwhile, John and Paul walked around the mall. Afterward, we ate lunch at a fast-food restaurant.

As we returned to the campground in the car, Lib told me how great the bathhouse was at the campground—like one's own private bathroom, clean and modern with lots of hot water. She had a key to it that I could borrow. I didn't have a key because I usually shower in our motorhome and didn't ask for one at the office.

In the afternoon and evening I napped and rested, taking three rounds of the cold medicine at the recommended times. I still had nasal congestion and a scratchy throat. After a nap on the sofa in the evening, I went to bed immediately, my eyes too tired to stay open.

Paul kept himself occupied with reading the newspaper and watching television with the sound muted. We never had to worry about John and Lib. They both were avid readers and had brought along books to occupy their leisure time. In addition, John bought a newspaper each day. Lib was also smocking (a kind of beautiful puckering embroidery) a child's dress that she had made for a friend.

Downtown Denver beckoned to us the next morning, Thursday, June 1. With my head reeling from the cold medicine, I decided to forgo taking more tablets that day. Yet I packed them into a small bag with cough drops and a full box of tissues for my cold symptoms.

In *sunshine* and a temperature of 62 degrees, we went in the tow car to the United States Mint at 320 West Colfax Avenue in Denver. We picked up free tickets at the ticket booth that was next to the visitors entrance on Cherokee Street. The ticket agents begin giving out tickets at eight o'clock in the morning for specific tour times and stop issuing them when all the tours have been filled for that day.

The Denver Mint, one of four in the United States, has operated since 1863. It produces circulating coins and specially issued coins. Its entire output of coins is distributed through Federal Reserve Banks according to shipping orders from the United States Mint in Washington, D.C. The Federal Reserve Banks send the coins on to their member banks.

We joined a tour group at 9:45 A.M. As we moved through the building, I saw that it was smaller and more old-fashioned than I had envisioned. From a platform, I looked down onto a large room with punch presses, shakers, and other machines and saw coins being made as well as the men and women whose daily job it was to be among all that coinage.

I tried to sense what it must be like to go to work at the mint each day, whether it would make a difference in how I spent my personal money. The people seemed to be going about their work with competence, looking up occasionally at the tourists looking down at them.

Our tour ended in a sales area where a variety of mint products had been packaged in handsome presentations. Paul and I bought a silver-dollar money clip for our son, Jeff.

From the mint, we walked toward the state capitol building, its gold-leafed, windowed dome gleaming in the sunshine. We posed for a picture while standing on the marker on its front steps that indicates an elevation of one mile above sea level, thus giving Denver its "Mile High City" label.

Inside the cavernous building, Lib and I admired a temporary display of 300 handmade quilts hanging on various levels of the multistoried building. Paul and John climbed narrow, winding stairs up to the dome interior, where they walked around the circular perimeter

"Paul and John climbed narrow, winding stairs up to the [state capitol] dome interior, where they walked around the circular perimeter and took pictures of the spectacular view of the city [Denver]."

and took pictures of the spectacular view of the city.

From the capitol, we walked several blocks to the 16th Street Mall, a mile-long promenade for pedestrians in the heart of Denver. We started to eat lunch outdoors at a restaurant but moved indoors because of the cool breeze that blew around our shaded table.

Following lunch, we walked three blocks east of the capitol to the Molly Brown House Museum at 1340 Pennsylvania Street. (Since parking in the Molly Brown House neighborhood is extremely tight, visitors are encouraged to use the ample parking spaces available in the capitol area.) The walk was worth it. We joined a small class of girls and the authentically costumed leader for a tour of the Victorian-style interior.

Molly Brown got her "Unsinkable" title and heroine reputation from her leadership during the *Titanic* disaster. She made the people in her lifeboat keep rowing, probably saving their lives. When she was asked how she survived, she reportedly said, "Typical Brown luck—we're unsinkable."

When we returned to the Graybeals' car, Paul used our cellular phone to call his sister Hazel to see if it was okay to visit that afternoon. She gave directions to Sedalia on U.S. 85 and then to Camp Colorado, which was another 15 miles southwest on Route 67 in Pike National Forest.

Although they formerly lived in Denver, Hazel never shared her husband's enthusiasm for Colorado and especially for the camp. She thought long and hard about being a camp co-manager. When asked why she decided to accept that role, her response was, "My husband loves Colorado and I love my husband." In spite of her mixed feelings, she tried to fulfill her obligations cheerfully and efficiently.

Al's enthusiasm for Colorado stemmed from his first visit during his college days when he attended a wedding in Denver. His enthusiasm for Camp Colorado emanated from his being a director for youth camps there when he was the pastor at the Prince of Peace Church in Denver. When the opportunity presented itself to be a camp manager, he was happy to accept the position.

Driving southwest from Sedalia, we eventually saw the brown sign with blue letters and the entrance to Camp Colorado on our left. Camp Colorado is owned by the Western Plains District of the Church of the Brethren. It draws campers from Colorado, Nebraska, Kansas, and New Mexico.

To our grateful surprise, we saw Al waiting for us and motioning to us from a golf-cart-style vehicle to follow him. How glad we were for his guidance on the one-way, narrow, dirt and gravel road that curved uphill and downhill to the camp buildings.

John parked the car in a dirt area near the Class C, 27-foot, cream-colored motorhome in which Al and Hazel had driven to Colorado. Paul, Lib, John, and I all emerged from the car into the cool air. The temperature must have been only in the 50s there in the foothills of the Rockies at an elevation of 7,500 feet.

Hazel warmly hugged Lib, Paul, and me, whom she knew, and shook hands with John, whom she was meeting for the first time. She wore a head scarf and a long-sleeved, three-quarter-length, bulky knitted gray cardigan over a blouse and skirt.

A graduate of the New England Conservatory of Music and an accomplished organist, Hazel had played the organ for many churches of various faiths including Churches of the Brethren, Methodist, Christian Church, Jewish (Conservative), Lutheran, Presbyterian, and the United Church of Christ.

Al is a retired minister of the Church of the Brethren, having served pastorates in Pennsylvania, Ohio, and Colorado. He was chaplain at the Woodville State Hospital, South Mountain Restoration Center, and Quincy United Methodist Home, all in Pennsylvania. In recent years, he had served as interim pastor at the Waynesboro Church of the Brethren in Pennsylvania and the Hagerstown Church of the Brethren in Maryland.

Smiling and dressed in work clothes—checked flannel shirt, jeans, zippered jacket, and baseball cap—Al enthusiastically showed us around the camp. It was about a week before the first campers were due to arrive and he still had plenty to do. Both he and Hazel were in their 70s.

The main camp building, a wooden lodge, was used for meals and group activities. Al led us up a steep incline to see a girls' cabin, the bathhouse, and then back down to the camp managers' cottage. There were nine buildings altogether, scattered about on the steep terrain, with uneven paths leading to each. They included three girls' cabins, three boys' cabins, the lodge, the managers' cabin, and a large recreation building with a maintenance shop beneath. The camp could accommodate 90 campers. We saw no frills anywhere; visitors could expect simple camping in the heart of forested hillsides.

At the end of the tour, the six of us settled into the living room area of the managers' cabin, which consisted of four rooms. In the large room at the front were a living room area and a dining/kitchen area. In the kitchen area were a dining room table and a desk made by Al. The desk, on which Hazel placed her computer equipment, had been fashioned of a door laid horizontally over columns of concrete blocks. The ancient gas stove had been replaced with a new one by the Guyers at their own expense. Two small bedrooms at the back of the cabin were separated by a very small bathroom and a camp supply storage closet that opened into a hallway between the bedrooms.

We shared stories about our trip, including our adventure from Durango to Grand Junction, and asked about their family and camp activities.

We found out that the camp serves the Church of the Brethren primarily but also rents to groups from other denominations and family groups, which brings campers from all over the United States. The camp calendar includes designated weeks for different-aged youths and adults plus times for family reunions. Planned activities are tailored to the particular group. The daily schedule for a ten-year-old camper, for example, during his or her week at camp includes eating meals in the lodge, taking turns helping to set the tables or clean up after meals, and cleaning up the cabin and bath facilities each morning. He or she would participate in activities such as Morning Watch (devotions), Bible study, hiking, crafts, games, vespers (evening devotions), and campfire circles.

Hazel and Al would be alone until the first campers arrived. Unfortunately, due to previous problems, the camp needed more cleaning and repair than usual. They had more than enough to do to get ready for the upcoming camping season. Al laughingly said he was "labor" and Hazel was "management." Already Al was working hard physically to improve the site and facilities.

During the camping season, Al would take the considerable pile of laundry that accumulated (including bed sheets for campers) each week to the laundromat at Castle Rock, about 25 miles south, empty the trash and garbage containers daily from the kitchen and bathrooms, keep supplies in stock and repair the bathrooms as needed, maintain the grading of the dirt and gravel road with a diesel tractor, and amidst all his other work, occasionally speak at a worship service. He would also fill in as a director of a family weekend camp as needed.

Later we learned that Hazel's responsibilities included making sure the camp was in compliance with all the regulations of the State Board of Health, answering the telephone and mail, making bank deposits and paying bills, ordering the food for each week's camp, and finding a professional roofer to replace the leaking roofs on the

"Hazel and Al would be alone until the first campers arrived. . . . They [as co-managers] had more than enough to do to get ready for the upcoming camping season." [L-R: the author, Hazel Guyer, Paul, Al Guyer]

lodge and the managers' cabin. She also selected the roofing materials and initiated and successfully led a fund-raising drive to pay for the work. Much to their satisfaction, the new roofs were completed the week before Hazel and Al closed the camp for the summer season and returned to their home in Pennsylvania. On her own, Hazel organized the registration, health, and financial records of the camp and compiled a six-page report outlining the responsibilities of the camp manager for future use. (Indeed it was later used to the ongoing enjoyment and appreciation of the trustees and succeeding camp managers alike at Camp Colorado.)

Referring to them as the "dynamic duo," the head trustee of Camp Colorado presented to Al and Hazel an "Excellence" plaque for their contributions to Camp Colorado as co-managers and fund raisers during their three and one-half months that summer. With its inscription on the right and a beautiful photograph with the viewer looking up through a group of Colorado's yellow-leaved aspen trees on the left, the oak plaque was the first such special recognition for a camp manager by the trustees.

What brave, enterprising, and dedicated people those two were! Hazel told me later that in spite of Al's getting very tired and her not wanting to be there, she actually enjoyed the camp at times, such as when she watched hummingbirds hover at the big hanging baskets of blooming petunias outside the managers' cabin.

All too soon, it was time for the Graybeals, Paul, and me to leave. As we drove away on the dirt road that led away from the camp, I looked down from the car and saw the small figure of Hazel waving to us from beside the lodge. She told me later that she had wished she could be going with us!

After that full day of sightseeing, I took a nap on the bed, ate some hot cereal, and took a second nap. About nine o'clock, I forced myself to knock on Lib's motorhome door to ask for the key to the campground bathhouse. I then enjoyed the luxury of a lingering shower in a large room with a chair on which I put my clothes and towel. The streams of soothing water improved my spirits if not my cold.

Now that we had accomplished our goal of visiting Hazel and Al at Camp Colorado, I was ready to see what else north-central Colorado had to offer its visitors and wondered whether we might somehow get to see Pikes Peak before leaving that intriguing state.

14

Pikes Peak Appears

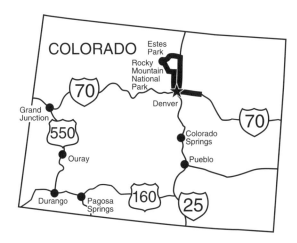

I DISCOVERED that in Colorado, a visitor can easily find a wide variety of exciting activities and spectacular sights whether staying two weeks or two months or, I would imagine, two years. The Graybeals and Paul and I had to choose what we wanted to do our final four days in Colorado.

We decided to head north in the car from Wheat Ridge, a Denver suburb, on that Friday, June 2, to visit Rocky Mountain National Park. The next day, Saturday, we wanted to take in the Denver Museum of Natural History. On Sunday, we would move our rigs to another campground on the east side of Denver where we would sightsee at the controversial, high-priced Denver airport. Then

Monday, we would leave Denver and head east toward Kansas. Some-where, somehow, I hoped we could see Pikes Peak.

My energy began to return, but a dry tickle in my throat and a cough continued. Cough drops were my mainstay.

As John drove the car northwest on the two-hour drive toward Estes Park, he and Paul conferred on what routes to take while Lib and I chatted in the back seat. Estes Park had been the site of the National Youth Conferences of our Church of the Brethren in 1962, 1978, 1982, and 1986. When the attendance became too great, the conferences were held at Fort Collins on the campus of Colorado State University in 1990, 1994, and 1998. I had heard people from our church talk about Estes Park and was curious to see it. Everyone said it was beautiful.

We rode slowly in the car through the town of Estes Park. It lay in a scenic valley at the very foot of the rugged, snow-topped Rocky Mountains. A warm, friendly, and unpretentious feeling reached out to me from the town. Its population of approximately 3,200 people gave it a delightful small-town ambiance. A combination of aspen trees, evergreens, and blooming flowers welcomed us.

Probably the only pretentious building was the Stanley Hotel. A white, four-storied, mansionlike, Georgian-style building overlook-ing the town, it was built by F. O. Stanley, who co-invented the Stanley Steamer automobile. Perhaps we could eat lunch there or at least visit it, I thought.

We headed first for the Rocky Mountain National Park at the edge of town. Outside the park, a sign told us that the road was closed up ahead. We realized we might not be able to drive the entire distance but wanted to go as far as possible.

John drove into the park and onto Trail Ridge Road. The hard-surfaced, two-lane road had a double yellow line down the middle and white lines on the edges with guardrails and caution signs where required. It was reputed to be the *highest* continuously paved high-way in the United States.

The elevations of the *valleys* in the park are about 8,000 feet, while its highest peak, Longs Peak, reaches 14,255 feet. The park as a whole encompasses about 266,000 acres of the Front Range of the Rocky Mountains.

Trail Ridge Road claims the highest mountain pass of the 37 passes in Colorado, Trail Ridge High Point, at an elevation of 12,183 feet, which occurs in Rocky Mountain National Park. The highest *peak* in Colorado is Mount Elbert, at 14,431 feet, in the Rocky mountain range.

We stopped at scenic overlooks. At one such stop, we joined a group of people listening to a park ranger tell about the bighorn sheep that grazed nearby along the edge of a small lake. Well beyond the lake, herds of elk came out of the forest to graze on the park hillsides.

When a road barrier prevented our going farther because the road was closed due to snow, we parked near a lookout point high in the mountains. Many other tourists gathered there, looking across a wide valley toward snowy mountain peaks in the distance. I took three successive photographs from left to right of the breathtaking

"When a road barrier prevented our going farther [into Rocky Mountain National Park] because the road [Trail Ridge Road] was closed due to snow, we parked near a lookout point high in the mountains. Many other tourists gathered there, looking across a wide valley toward snowy mountain peaks in the distance."

diorama with the thought that I may paint it as one scene when I got home. An artist in Silverton told Lib and me that that was the technique he had used to paint a beautiful nature scene we admired in his studio.

At the same lookout, a group of perhaps a dozen motorcyclists on Harley-Davidsons had stopped along with other tourists. Paul talked with several of them and learned that they were attending a national convention being held at the YMCA in Estes Park.

On our return descent, we saw many more elk and estimated that we had seen 100 total that day. In addition, we saw mule deer, ground squirrels, and several beaver lodges and dams.

Re-entering Estes Park, we left the main street, drove uphill, and parked beside the stately Stanley Hotel. We entered the well-kept, spacious, historic, high-ceilinged lobby, which contained an actual Stanley Steamer car like that co-invented by F. O. Stanley. Near the entry was the original 1909 Otis elevator. The woman at the front desk directed us to a dining room, where we enjoyed the lunch fare.

"Re-entering Estes Park, we left the main street, drove uphill, and parked beside the stately Stanley Hotel. We entered the well-kept, spacious, historic, high-ceilinged lobby, which contained an actual Stanley Steamer car like that co-invented by F. O. Stanley."

Afterward we wandered about, looking into three large meeting rooms. We admired the chandeliers and wood-framed fireplaces in two of them. I picked up a "Tariff Schedule" from the hotel desk and learned that the hotel offered various styles and sizes of suites and guest rooms, at various prices, of course. Outside from the broad, landscaped terrace in front of the huge, U-shaped, white complex, I looked down at the town of Estes Park and the Rocky Mountains beyond.

Even in the misty rain, we could not resist browsing the shopping feast that Estes Park offered. Lib and I wandered in and out of the numerous arts and crafts, jewelry, and clothing shops on the main street and beyond. Paul and John browsed and shopped on their own. Among other purchases, Lib and I each bought a pair of aspen leaf earrings, gold-plated for her and silver-plated for me. Beneath the plating were actual leaves from aspen trees.

On our way back from beautiful Estes Park to the campground, John pulled into the Rocky Mountain Antiques mall. We all piled out, including Paul, who was thereby initiated into antique shopping. We roamed among the exceptionally clean, enormous room of inviting antiques and collectibles.

We had started out that morning under sunny skies, but on the way back to the campground on U.S. 34 east of Loveland, we encountered hail. Farther toward Denver on I-25, we saw lightning in the distance, but it remained far away from us.

Back at the campground in the motorhome, Paul prepared his own supper while I napped. About 6:30, I took a pain reliever caplet for a throbbing headache, ate half of a sandwich, watched some television, and went to bed hoping my cold would be gone the next day.

On Saturday, June 3, our 18th day on the road, my head throbbed and any physical exertion caused shortness of breath. The headache and having to consciously breathe deeply made it difficult for me to do anything but essentials.

Lib, John, and Paul went in the car to a camping store and the grocery store. I stayed behind in the motorhome to write a few postcards, to catch up on writing in my spiral tablet, and to have some time to relax and recuperate from the cold. I was too fatigued to read or listen to writing tapes.

I took another pain reliever caplet about 11:00. I would be glad when we got down out of the high altitude! I just knew it was reducing my energy. I struggled to keep a positive outlook, but I couldn't think as clearly as normal. I wondered how other people got used to the altitude. I decided that I may have had a harder time adjusting because I breathed in a more shallow fashion than many people. It was unusual for me to feel the way I did and a little scary. Now I saw why a good friend suffering with a heart condition became almost panicky without his extra oxygen during his illness.

As I wrote in my spiral tablet and looked at my log, I realized that so far on the trip, we had had only three sunny days! At that moment, it was cloudy, about 62 degrees, and breezy. I had the door and opposite window open for fresh air. I was so weak and shaky from just writing in the tablet that I stopped and lay down on the sofa.

I was glad that Paul, at least, was in good spirits, feeling well, and enjoying our stay in Wheat Ridge.

In the afternoon, I was feeling somewhat better and pushed myself to join the others in sightseeing. We stopped to pick up Paul's shoes at the repair shop before driving to the Denver Museum of Natural History at 2001 Colorado Boulevard. The entrance to the modern facility, one of the largest such museums in the United States, was busy with scores of other visitors. Inside it offered a plethora of exhibits and activities. We bought tickets for the 3:00 P.M. showing of *Yellowstone* in the IMAX® theater.

While we waited for the movie to start, Lib and John decided to roam the gem and minerals exhibit while Paul and I headed for "Explore Colorado: From Plains to Peaks." I marveled at the glass-enclosed dioramas of Colorado's diverse ecosystems, which showed wildlife in their natural habitats. All too soon, it was time to head for the theater in the same building.

The four of us met on the second floor and filed into the theater, which boasted a screen four and one-half stories tall and sound that surrounded viewers. The film *Yellowstone,* a travelogue with beautiful scenery of Yellowstone National Park and the Yellowstone River, included scenes of pre-Colombian people and early Europeans in the area of the river. The huge, brilliant images on the screen captivated me, at times making me feel a part of the action.

Afterward, the four of us viewed other exhibits in the museum. I paid close attention to one titled "North American Indian Cultures." Once again I saw shiny black sculptures like the one my long-lost pen pal had sent to me.

There was so much more to see—ancient peoples, prehistoric animals, Egyptian mummies, rare birds, and the planet itself in the planetarium, as well as watching other breathtaking films, such as *Titanica*. One could spend weeks admiring and learning from the accurate and excellent presentations about the natural world.

Downstairs on the main level, in the gift shop, Paul and I bought a Barlow brass letter opener with an ivory scrimshaw inlay in the handle. It would be another gift for Jeff's December birthday.

After leaving the museum, John drove us to downtown Denver to McCormick's Fish House & Bar, at 1659 Wazee, for a special Saturday night dinner. Recommended as the best seafood restaurant in Denver, it was located in the historic district in the old Oxford Hotel. Not recognizing the main entrance, we walked through a lively bar into a large hallway near the main dining room. While we stood in the hallway waiting to be seated, servers hurried past us into other dining areas carrying trays of food at shoulder height.

When we were seated in the wood-paneled main dining room, a waiter dressed in a white shirt and jacket with black trousers and black bow tie soon came and took our orders. Later as he refilled our water goblets, we gasped, marveled, then laughed at his technique. He nonchalantly held the water pitcher high, high in the air above each goblet, letting the water run down like a waterfall as he refilled it, never spilling a drop.

From our oversized menu, we not only ordered our food but also read a little history of the place. Of special interest was that in the early 1970s, Peter, Paul, and Mary sang their famous "Blowin' in the Wind" there and John Denver his "Rocky Mountain High."

In spite of my cold, I enjoyed the museum and meal. Back at the motorhome, Paul read the newspaper and watched television and I went to bed early. Our time in Denver was coming to a close. We had not seen Pikes Peak, but what an array of other marvels of nature and humanity we had seen! The next day we would move our caravan to the east side of Denver.

At 10:42 A.M., on Sunday, June 4, the four of us left Prospect RV Park & Campground, Wheat Ridge, in our motorhomes. We headed to the east side of Denver for one night's stay. While there we hoped to visit the new Denver International Airport, our last major sightseeing stop in Colorado. Even though we were too far away to travel to the top of Pikes Peak, I had not given up the hope of seeing that famous monument from a distance. Although the peak is about 65 miles south of Denver, I had been told that it was visible from some places in the Denver area.

Earlier that cloudy morning, Paul had dumped our gray and black water tanks. We had watched a worship service on the television. (I had, of course, had my usual Bible reading and prayer time before breakfast.)

As I thought about our trip to that point, I realized that Paul and John had always registered us at campgrounds while Lib and I stayed in our respective motorhomes waiting. When they went to register, John and Paul discussed the number of nights to stay. This system worked well and suited me just fine, and I imagine Lib also.

When Paul and I travel alone, I often register for us while he stays behind the wheel and keeps the motorhome motor running. Whoever registers has to decide whether to get full hookups (water, electricity, and sewer) or just water and electricity. Sometimes we discuss this before registering. Usually the full hookup costs more. Sometimes there's no choice—all sites have full hookups. When a campground offers only water and electricity at campsites, it has a dump station that a camper may use without paying an extra fee. Some campgrounds charge extra fees of perhaps $2 per day for electricity, which we pay when we plan to use the air conditioner in warm weather or an electric heater in winter. Cable television hookups usually cost extra, at least $2 per day.

Campground fees range from about $12 to $30, depending on the location and amenities. I read in a motorhoming magazine of a campground in California that offers a "supersite"—with a privacy fence and locked gate with a key for the camper, a paved patio that includes a washer and dryer and outdoor furniture, a hot tub, and a gas barbecue—for $300 for a summer weekend. Fees at upscale RV parks such as some at Disney World in Florida can be as much as $59 per night depending on the season and the vacation package purchased. With more than 16,000 public and private campgrounds in the United States, RVers have lots of choices.

Thinking further about our traveling together in a two-RV caravan, I realized that John and Paul both observed posted speed limits and drove with safety in mind, both in the motorhome and tow car. Both men were excellent drivers.

John had an uncanny sense and keen vision for locating street signs; Lib assisted in reading maps, making them a team of excellent navigators. They both took the time and made the effort to discover what was offered at each destination and along the way, such as the Denver Museum of Natural History yesterday. They kept learning and enjoying themselves.

Although previously reluctant to stop along the way for museums, Paul had enjoyed all of the sightseeing on our Colorado trip. He had been very amenable to what John and Lib had suggested to see and do.

An hour later, our RVs turned into the KOA Denver East, Strasburg, Colorado. Once more Paul registered us, this time for one night.

With lunch and the afternoon before us, the four of us decided to go to the airport that day instead of the next morning. I had read a food critic's review in *The Denver Post* of the 52 restaurants at the airport; it concluded with a recommendation for Lefty's Mile High Grill on Concourse B, east wing.

Off we went in the tow car. Soon the architecture of the Denver International Airport drew us closer. The 34 white fabric peaks of

Jeppesen Terminal, the airport's terminal, looked like Colorado's snowcapped Rocky Mountains or an enormous big-top circus tent. Either way, they attracted tourists. The terminal was named for Elrey Jeppesen, an aviation pioneer from Colorado.

A 53-square-mile airport, built at a cost of $4.2 billion, it had five full-service runways and was built with room to expand. Parking was in two five-level parking garages—one on the east side of the terminal and the other on the west side—each with 6,500 spaces not more than 750 feet from the terminal.

What fun to explore the enormous terminal! It offered escalators, elevators, moving walkways, and even a subwaylike train so that people did not have to walk long distances. An automated voice in the bustling Jeppesen Terminal announced the arrival of the underground train going to Concourse B, which is where the restaurants were located. Once we were on the modern train, the same soothing, feminine voice announced our stop at Concourse B.

We stepped from the train out into the enormous concourse with shops on both sides. In the middle of the area, running as far as the eye could see, were two long lengths of people movers, slowly carrying standing folks to their destinations.

We had no idea where to find Lefty's restaurant, but with all of us looking and asking, we eventually saw it. Soon we sat eating at a table by a window that overlooked the tarmac. Planes arrived, got serviced, and departed as we watched.

Later we browsed in gift shops. In one shop, between a display of tee shirts and a rack of CDS, I heard an old-time version of "Home on the Range" being played by a guitar. I lingered to listen. It sounded like the Western music that radio singers such as Gene Autry used to sing. Making sure the same artist and song were on a CD on display called *The Wild West*, I couldn't resist buying one. A gold medallion on the cover said that it received the Western Heritage Wrangler Award from the National Cowboy Hall of Fame and Western Heritage Center.

On the floor of the giant concourse on our way back to the car, we saw a tiny gray mouse, no bigger than a chicken egg. It darted first one way and then another, seemingly not knowing which way to go. We left it to its own devices. How it got in there we did not know.

In the car, leaving the airport, I asked John if we could stop somewhere so that I could take a picture of the marvel of modern architecture and design that we had just experienced. True to form, he pulled over at just the right spot so that I could get a good shot of the white peaks of the terminal.

Back at the motorhome, I realized that we had accomplished our two main goals for that day: to set up camp on the east side of Denver and to see the new airport. The next day, we would head eastward toward home. It looked as if we would have to forgo Pikes Peak, but I stubbornly held out hope for a glimpse of it on our way out of the Denver area.

After a light supper, I did the dishes while Paul went outside to clean the windshield, headlights, and taillights. He checked the various oil levels and used the pressure gauge to be sure each tire had sufficient air, including the spare, of course. I wrote a few postcards then rested on the bed so that Paul, who by then had finished his outside activities, could stretch out on the sofa and watch television. My cold was getting better, but I continued to have to consciously breathe deeply. I didn't yet have the extra energy to go for a walk that evening on the campground road.

As I lay with my eyes closed, I realized that the spiral tablet in which I had been writing notes of the trip was full, so I got up to find the second one that I had brought along. I laid it on the carpeted hump beside the passenger seat. I sat down in the easy chair across from the sofa and asked Paul if I could turn up the sound on the television.

"Of course," he said.

In bright sunshine, Paul unhooked our motorhome from the campground's electric and water supply on Monday morning, June 5, day 20 of our Colorado trip. The clear day meant that we might have a chance to see Pikes Peak yet. The four of us left the KOA Denver

East campground about 7:30 A.M. and traveled east on I-70. John's voice came over the CB.

"Mountains at nine o'clock."

Mountains all along the horizon looked like travel brochure pictures. It was the best view of mountains we had had in Colorado, mainly because there had been only three sunny days so far the whole trip—the day we left Maryland, the day we entered Colorado, and the day we visited downtown Denver and Camp Colorado. I had a sinking feeling about all the beautiful views we had missed because of rain, snow, hail, sleet, and haze, yet we had seen much splendor.

Although the altitude adjustments had proved challenging, I felt sad about leaving Colorado. It was a place of beauty and adventure, and our trip would be over soon.

At mile marker 311 on I-70 just beyond Strasburg, Colorado, John again came on the CB.

"I believe the view ahead is different from the views we've seen the last two weeks."

Ahead lay a wide, almost level, sweep of landscape as far as I could see as I turned my head left and right. Only occasional electric poles or buildings intruded on the skyline.

"Well, there is a mountain over there," I said to Paul as I swiveled my chair and turned my head farther to the right. I squinted my eyes. I saw the top of a beautiful snowy mountain low on the horizon. It seemed to shout to me from a great distance away toward the southwest.

"Could—could it be Pikes Peak?" I asked Paul, almost holding my breath.

Quickly, I reached for a booklet I had bought in Colorado Springs. I compared what I saw outside our motorhome window with photographs of the massive, rounded, high peak. I located on the state map where the mountain was relative to where we were on I-70. It *was* Pikes Peak!

Just as Alaska had treated us to its resplendent Mount McKinley in full sunshine, so Colorado could not let us go without at least a fleeting glimpse of its most famous, magnificent peak. It shone in all its glory in the sunlight.

Of course, I regretted not being able to ascend to the top when we were actually there, either by cog railway or by car, because of snowy weather conditions. But I had had at least a peek at Pikes Peak! And I was satisfied.

Now I could head east, mission accomplished, as I looked forward to visiting the home of Mark Twain, two days away.

15

Mark Twain's Boyhood Home and Museum

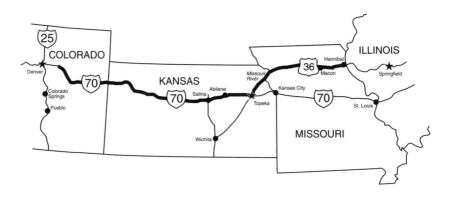

DURING THE EXCITEMENT of seeing the gleaming white crown of Pikes Peak in the distance, our motorhomes continued east from Denver on that Monday morning, June 5, on I-70 with the Graybeals in the lead. I settled down in my passenger seat and enjoyed thinking that one day before we reached home we would see the boyhood home of a famous literary figure, Mark Twain, in Hannibal, Missouri.

"I enjoyed the last two weeks, but I'm not ready to turn around and do it again right away," John's voice came over the CB. He was referring to the unforeseen weather delays we had experienced on our Memorial Day trek from Durango to Grand Junction.

I asked Paul, "Where are we headed today?"

"Into Kansas," he replied matter-of-factly.

John's voice came over the CB. "Off to the right, little deer with white bellies."

As they had done on the Alaskan trip, John and Lib alerted us to any wild animals that they saw as they traveled ahead of us so that we could enjoy seeing them, too. We looked in time to see the deer running across a grassy field.

By 8:55 A.M., the outside temperature had risen from about 50 degrees when we left the campground to near 80 degrees. John and Paul pulled onto the wide shoulder of I-70 to change from long trousers to shorts, leaving the engines running. I changed from long blue denim pants into taupe pantyhose and white Bermuda shorts that went with my short-sleeved red knit top and white tennis shoes.

More comfortable, the men drove on.

"Milkweed! About four deer off on the right! *We* just passed them," exclaimed John, who was at least the length of a football field ahead of us.

"Now there are one, two, three, four on the left—by the railroad track," John said by CB.

"We see them. Thank you," Paul said.

Since the passenger seat was in full sunlight, I moved back onto the shaded sofa behind the driver's seat, where I lounged with my back propped up against pillows, my legs stretched out in front of me on the sofa, and facing forward.

"Wide open prairie has its beauty, too, doesn't it?" commented Paul to John on the CB.

"Sure does . . . " From my sofa seat, I did not hear the rest of what John said.

"What speed are you going?" I asked Paul. I had just seen a sign that said the speed limit in Colorado was 65 miles per hour, yet it seemed to me that we were going slower than our usual 55 miles per hour.

"He's been running around 50, but I think that's pretty much because of the rough, bumpy roads."

"Rest area coming up. Want to stop? Next one is 39 miles," asked John by CB. Some rest areas we stopped at, others we didn't, but John checked with us whenever one came along. We declined that time.

My cold was much better that day. I was getting my energy back. I had not coughed so far and my congestion had waned.

"Going to pick it up to 55 so traffic doesn't get too upset with me," John said, referring to his speed.

Since we left Strasburg two hours earlier, we had seen miles and miles of low hills and grasslands that hosted occasional herds of cattle. By midmorning, the highway was flanked by huge fields sprouting young, green blades of grain.

As we left Colorado and entered Kansas, John said, "Farewell to Colorado. Two weeks ago today! Fourteen nights in Colorado."

"I really liked Colorado." I said to Paul. "Did you?"

"Yes," he replied. "I can honestly say that it was enjoyable. The scenery was excellent."

Barely into Kansas, one farmer reminded passersby with a sign: "1 Kansas farmer feeds 92 people like you."

"Well, sure looks like Kansas, doesn't it?" I said, gazing out at the farmland.

"I would say," Paul answered.

The interstate cut between wide fields, some newly cultivated, some with growing grain. I could picture great modern combines later moving across these areas, reaping and baling.

"It's beautiful—the sky is beautiful," I said. Small cottony puffs were randomly grouped low on the horizon with blue sky above. They looked like a heavenly city of small white and gray fluffy clouds.

As we drove through the level fields of Kansas, my mind lighted up with memories of our visits on the way out to Colorado. I sensed again an increased admiration for our former presidents Truman and Eisenhower. I admired their courage and risk-taking in going from small-town roots to big-city politics while maintaining their Mid-western values.

That Monday drive turned out to be a full day's travel. At 4:51 late that afternoon, we arrived at Triple J RV Park, Russell, Kansas, birthplace of Bob Dole, former United States senator and Republican candidate for president. While Paul registered in the campground office, I used that time to look at the odometer and write our mileage in the trip log. I calculated that we had driven 342 miles that day. The sun shone and our outside thermometer read 81 degrees.

At the campsite assigned to us, Paul hooked up to the water and electricity. Soon the four of us walked along a gravel road from the campground to South Highway 281 in Russell. We settled in at Meridy's Restaurant & Lounge for dinner. Its specialty was "great steaks," and John wanted one last good steak while in the West.

Afterward, we walked back on the gravel road to our motorhome. There the four of us eased into the dinette seats and played four games of Rummikub®. I thought of the birthday party we had had for Paul on the way out to Colorado. The party atmosphere continued that night in Russell. John wanted to get proficient enough at Rummikub® to have a fair shot at winning when introducing the game to his grandchildren. They are one bright group of children in my opinion and apparently his, too. He won two games out of the four that we played, so we pronounced him ready for his young kin. Lib won one game and Paul the other. I won zilch!

That day had been the fourth sunny day out of 20 so far on the trip. We didn't take it for granted!

The next morning, as Paul and I went through our usual morn-ing rituals, which included getting our own breakfasts, we ended up ready to eat at the same time at the dinette table. Paul prayed the blessing aloud as is our custom, and in my mind I added grateful thanks for the lower elevation in Kansas and the healing that was tak-ing place within me. I knew that the next time I traveled to high ele-vations such as the mountains of Colorado, I would schedule time to acclimate my body to the thinner air. I knew, too, that I needed to stay in good physical shape at home by exercising regularly. That would be easy because I love to walk. Behind our home is a lovely, wooded road that is both convenient and pleasant for walking. When the weather is too cold, I can go to the mall in town or even walk inside the house.

In breezy, cloudy, muggy, 60-degree weather at 8:07 A.M., our little troop moved out of the Triple J Campground in Russell, Kansas, on day 21, Tuesday, June 6, for a full day's travel across the remaining five-eighths of Kansas and into Missouri. Our next major sight to see was Mark Twain's home in Hannibal, Missouri, but not that day. We had many miles to go first.

We drove on I-70 with John and Lib at least a football-field length ahead of our vehicle. A gray fox suddenly came out of the tall grass on our right. As it ran across our lane toward the median strip, a car ahead of us hit it. It lay lifeless on the left shoulder of our lane. It was a sobering moment.

About nine o'clock, as we traveled I-70 toward Salina, Kansas, I got out my laptop computer and began tapping the keys.

"Rest area about one mile. Next one about 40-some miles," John's voice came over the CB.

"I wouldn't mind stopping at this one, please," Paul returned.

"Okay. Will do."

Soon we saw the rest area sign and, following the Graybeals, veered onto a ramp leading into a well-planned parking area. Parked cars slanted toward the curb; a median strip of grass demarcated parallel parking for larger vehicles like ours. A pioneer-style, stone-faced building with chimneys on either side and a sloped shingle roof accommodated rest rooms. Other amenities included outside trash containers, roofed picnic tables, telephones, and a *USA Today* newspaper stand, all in a country motif.

Besides stopping to use the rest room, many RVers use rest areas to stretch their legs by walking around outside. They may look for anything unusual about the tires or the rig, chat with truck drivers or other RVers, walk the dog in the pet area, buy a newspaper if available, get travel answers and printed materials at the information center, eat a snack, look at a map, make a call from a public telephone, or switch drivers. Some rest areas even provide dump stations and sites for RV parking overnight.

As we continued on I-70, muggy humidity clouded whatever scenery was in the distance.

"Milkweed. Buffalo herd on the right," John announced on the CB.

"Guess there were about 12 in that herd," Paul said after we passed.

"At least!" I said. One lone bison stood completely still while all the others lay in the grass like huge clumps of brown clothes. At one of the exhibits in the Denver Museum of Natural History I had read that bison use so much energy when they move that they often stand still, but when they run, they can go as fast as 35 miles an hour.

During the time that I had had my cold, it was all I could do to fight the virus and the high altitude. I did not do any work at the computer but jotted notes in my spiral tablet. I was glad to have the chance now to catch up on my writing in the computer.

I was sure my cold germ had come from a man who cleared his throat heartily as he walked past me and my plate of food in the restaurant in Silverton, Colorado, the day we rode the narrow gauge railroad from Durango. That was Sunday; by Tuesday the symptoms had appeared.

"The elevation at Russell, Kansas, was 1,826," I said to Paul after looking it up in the AAA TourBook® guide. "Ah-h-h," I sighed and then breathed in the oxygen-laden air, relieved to be down from the heights in the Rockies.

"That's more of what you're used to at home," Paul said.

As we continued east, I said to Paul, "You know something? It looks like this grain is getting ripe!" Enormous fields had a yellow cast.

"It's more so than the green we saw back there," Paul said, referring to fields we had seen earlier in the day.

Some fields looked wet and I saw mud in unplanted ground. Ponds were brimful.

I continued typing into my computer as we drove along and simultaneously looked out at the scenery. I thought about my eating habits on the trip. When we were busy sightseeing, I hadn't eaten as much. (Also, my weight had decreased during my cold as I experienced a loss of appetite.) That said to me that when I was at home, I was eating snacks from boredom. With all that we were seeing and doing, snacking had lost its priority for me. I had not usually eaten a snack before going to bed on the trip as I would have at home. While riding along, I had written into the computer or taken notes in the spiral tablet. Those tasks had occupied my mind. Sometimes I had listened to tapes from the Philadelphia Christian Writers Conference. When I had snacked, I ate two or three tiny pretzels.

While we're on the subject of boredom, once a woman called into a talk radio show on which I was being interviewed and asked what to do to keep from being bored when she was riding in an RV. I had not had that problem myself, but I thought of the different activities that people do besides enjoying the scenery—doing handiwork such as knitting and crocheting, listening to audio books borrowed from a library, listening to the radio, playing games that don't distract the driver, writing in a journal, and browsing tour guides and maps. The chief deterrent to boredom is staying active even though sitting in the passenger seat. For example, if Paul asks for a soda or even a neck rub, I get up from my seat and fulfill those requests; sometimes I even suggest them myself. Sitting still and putting off doing an activity creates fatigue and boredom.

"We haven't come to Salina yet, have we?" I asked Paul.

"No. According to that last sign I saw, it ought to be about nine more miles," Paul said.

I read in the AAA TourBook® guide that the elevation of Salina is 1,222 feet, and Topeka is only 950 feet. Was I glad to be back down to earth! Although I really enjoyed Colorado, its altitude had bothered me much more than I had expected.

We glided ahead on I-70. Several miles beyond Salina toward Abilene, as we crossed the Solomon River, John said, "The river's been out of its bank a little bit." A "little bit" was an understatement because a whole, large field near the river looked muddy and saturated with water. As I examined the field, the sun shone briefly and then was quietly cloaked by passing clouds.

As we entered Abilene's city limits, John said, "We put on 1,645 miles from Abilene to Abilene," referring to our loop west and back again. The Telephony Museum, the Kirby House, and the Eisenhower Center in Abilene had intrigued us two and a half weeks earlier. This time we simply drove through Abilene en route to Macon, Missouri.

"Topeka, 80 miles," Paul said, reading a sign at midmorning.

"They have really had some water," Paul said as we looked at a large, soaked field of young grain, some of which was washed out.

I took time out from writing to get Paul some Diet Sprite and a handful of small pretzels. I handed him the almost empty plastic bottle of soda that he had placed in the refrigerator when we were in Colorado. The sides of the bottle were sucked inward. As soon as Paul screwed off the lid, the sides returned to their normal round shape. It was a demonstration that greater air pressure exists at lower elevations.

In eastern Kansas, evidence of excessive rain and flooding continued to draw our sympathy.

"Flat land flooded in there," Paul said to me, referring to a field we were passing.

"Yes, yes." How sad to see the young shoots of grain destroyed by recent floodwaters.

In Topeka, the capital of Kansas, John came on the CB to call our attention to the capitol building on our right. I saw a high dome in the distance towering above other buildings. A guidebook reminded me that Topeka is the home of the renowned Menninger Clinic.

We left I-70 at Topeka, Kansas, and took Route 4/U.S. 59 northeast to St. Joseph, Missouri, where we traveled on U.S. 36 East.

Paul preferred to concentrate on driving rather than have the dash radio on. The CB didn't bother him, however; in fact, sometimes he listened to it with earphones. That left me free to listen to tapes on a small tape recorder with earphones, which I did as we rode along that day.

After 394 miles, we arrived at Shoemaker's RV Park, Bevier (near Macon), Missouri, at 4:57 P.M. in sunshine. When John and Paul registered at the campground office, they learned that the park could not provide water that night. Road construction workers had struck a water main that day in the area of our campground.

When Paul told me, I thought he had heard wrong. That was the first time we found a campground with a water problem, but of course it was not the owner's fault. We could have gone on to another campground, I suppose, but the fellows thought we could manage with our on-board supplies. Besides, they had already driven almost 400 miles that day.

The monitor panel located inside the motorhome above the entry door indicated that our fresh water tank was one-fourth full. The tank capacity was 65 gallons. That meant we had about 16 gallons to use. Because water weighs about eight pounds per gallon, we usually did not carry a full tank with us on the road unless we knew we would be dry camping. Fortunately, we kept three gallons of drinking water in plastic gallon jugs and refilled them as needed. Nevertheless, we would have to conserve water—no showers that night.

While John and Paul hooked up the motorhomes to electricity, Libby and I discussed whether to eat in or out.

"The fellows have had a big day," said Libby.

"Paul wants to eat in," I said. And so we ate in our individual motorhomes.

I prepared the ingredients from a box of Betty Crocker® Three Cheese Casserole, added a can of short asparagus spears, and followed the microwave instructions. Delicious! With the casserole I served applesauce and rolls. For dessert, Paul had vanilla pudding while I ate one SnackWell's® creme-filled cookie.

That evening, as Lib and I walked the campground roads, swarms of mosquitoes greeted us. We'd found none of those in Colorado. It had been too cold! When we battled snow in Colorado, we should have remembered the blessing of no mosquitoes.

Paul and John toured the mini-museum at the campground, looking at a 1931 Chevrolet coupe and a 1948 Ford, group pictures of army and navy men, small navy ship models, a few eight-foot-long navy ship models, and other naval memorabilia. The campground owner told Paul that they were having the wettest May on record in that area.

Before retiring for the evening, the four of us stood talking between our parked motorhomes.

"What time shall we leave tomorrow morning, John?" I asked.

John reached into the driver's seat area of their motorhome and retrieved a piece of scrap paper. I looked at his handwriting on the white paper and saw his plans for the next day. When he had had time to figure them out and write them down confounded me. He suggested going to Hannibal, Missouri, the next morning to take in the Mark Twain home, then traveling 115 miles to Springfield, Illinois, where we would camp. At Springfield, we would look for a mall where I could get my hair done and then sightsee the Abraham Lincoln site. Bless John! I had mentioned earlier that I would like to find a hairdresser in the next day or so.

"Eightish should be fine," answered John.

We each disappeared into our motorhomes for the night.

As Paul and I watched television in our motorhome, the screen went blank. After doing some testing with a voltmeter that he always carries in the RV, Paul determined that the electric outlet we used for the television and videocassette recorder was defective. He would repair it at home. Meanwhile, we used an extension cord to plug the television and VCR into another outlet and watched until after the first segment of the 10:00 news. We then went to sleep.

Chirps, tweets, and caws—a multitude of them—awoke me early the next morning, Wednesday, June 7. In Colorado in the morning, we had heard highway traffic in Pueblo, the Durango-Silverton train in Durango, people talking and walking in Wheat Ridge, but no birds that I remembered. I had missed hearing them.

That morning in Bevier, Missouri, their cacophonic yet sweet-sounding chorus permeated the campground. One particular noise made me sit up in bed to listen. It sounded like the beep of the cellular phone when the battery needed recharging. No, it was a bird. And I lay down again until the alarm squealed a half-hour later at 6 A.M.

That was the day for Mark Twain, my hairdo, and Abraham Lincoln. I wondered if we would really do everything all on the same day as John had planned. I was particularly excited that Mark Twain's Boyhood Home was on our itinerary that morning.

After breakfast, I asked Paul if he would help me raise the platform bed so that I could see how much water was in the fresh water tank that lay beneath. There had been times in the past when the gauge above the entry door did not give a true reading. We were both surprised to see that the tank was half-full of water. I decided to take a shower but was mindful of not using too much water. How refreshing it was even so!

By "eightish," we journeyed on U.S. 36 toward Hannibal, Missouri. With the Graybeals moving ahead at 55 miles per hour, we passed a sign: "Hannibal, 62 miles."

The sun shone; the temperature was in the low 70s. Behind the steering wheel, Paul wore dark amber sunglasses, a white short-sleeved shirt with dark blue pinstripes, and navy Bermuda shorts. In the passenger seat, I wore a splashy, multicolored, short-sleeved blouse with matching skort (a combination of a skirt and shorts) and fabric belt, and silver-and-pearl dangling earrings. The laptop computer sat on a towel-wrapped board on my lap. I had discovered that the towel helped to keep the board anchored in the glove compartment and softened its impact on my lap.

Paul reached in front of him and turned on the generator switch located on the dash. Immediately, we heard the zoomlike sound of the generator motor turning over. The generator helped to provide electrical energy for the overhead air conditioner that blew cool air toward us. Ever since I learned the function of the auxiliary generator, I have thought of it as my special friend. It allows us to operate electrical appliances when we are not hooked up to campground electricity. When we were stranded in the snow on Coal Bank Hill, I was glad that the generator was part of the motorhome. When we were wilderness camping in Alaska, I was grateful for the generator so that

I could cook food for a group potluck supper in the microwave/convection oven.

The auxiliary generator does not make electricity itself. Rather, it *converts* mechanical energy into electrical energy that flows through the motorhome's outlets and powers the air conditioner and other electrical appliances. The generator uses gasoline from the same tank as the engine.

Our motorhome has a safety feature that cuts off the flow of gasoline to the generator when the gas tank is less than one-fourth full. The idea is to always have enough gasoline in the tank to start the motorhome engine to get to a gasoline filling station before the tank becomes empty. Paul has a rule whereby he never lets the gasoline in the tank get below one-fourth full. If we are in an area that has few filling stations, he keeps the gasoline level above the one-half mark in the tank.

"Squirrel on the road!" John said from his vantage point well ahead of us.

Sure enough, a squirrel crossed ahead of us. Paul tooted the horn and the squirrel scurried faster, giving a great leap over tall grass at the side of the road.

"I gave him a little audible help," Paul said smiling over the CB to John.

"I did, too, and he went back to the left, thank goodness," said John.

I was glad the squirrel did not suffer the same fate as the gray fox we had seen the day before.

The countryside looked saturated. A railroad track paralleled our two-lane road. The sun had not yet burned off the morning haze, but it did cast shadows. We passed a muddy river flowing out of its banks.

"How are you feeling about the trip so far?" I asked Paul.

"Fine," he said quickly and definitely. "How about you?"

"Oh—fine, too. I think it's one of the nicest trips we've had."

"Pretty nice, I think. No long departure meetings," Paul said, referring to our "trip of a lifetime" to Alaska with an RV caravan. He was not complaining, just commenting.

My cold hung on, but overall I felt much better, especially at the lower altitude.

At 9:10 A.M. we arrived in Hannibal and parked the motorhomes in the Steamboat Bend Shopping Center. Soon John and Lib had unhooked the tow car and we all climbed inside—destination: Mark Twain's Boyhood Home, 208 Hill Street, where Samuel Clemens lived between the ages of 7 and 17.

The life of Mark Twain, the pseudonym for Samuel Langhorne Clemens, engrossed me as I walked into the ivy-covered museum and the adjoining boyhood home and across the brick-laid street to the home of Becky Thatcher. Samuel Clemens modeled his characters in *The Adventures of Tom Sawyer* after family and friends: Tom Sawyer—himself; Becky Thatcher—Laura Hawkins, his childhood sweetheart; and Aunt Polly—his mother.

First, after buying tickets in the museum, we saw a video of Samuel Clemens's life. Then we walked around the museum, examining memorabilia that included original manuscripts, first editions of Clemens's books, photographs, and the very desk that he used when writing *The Adventures of Tom Sawyer.*

His adjoining boyhood home was a simple, two-story house with white siding. Looking at it from the front, I saw two windows on either side of an entry door on the first floor and three windows on the second floor. Inside the house, I stood at the doorway of the kitchen where, in Clemens's imagination, Tom Sawyer stole a doughnut from a cupboard of Aunt Polly's kitchen. Upstairs, I saw Clemens's bedroom with its four-poster bed and rope "springs."

Outside, a new wooden fence adjoined the boyhood home and stood on the location of the one that had inspired the whitewashing story in which Tom's friends paid him with marbles and other items for the privilege of letting them paint it. I touched the white board fence twice, even though it was not the original, and took a picture of Pal, Lib, and John in front of it.

We walked across the street and up the steps into Becky Thatcher's (Laura Hawkins's) house, which had been turned into a bookstore.

"I touched the white board fence twice, even though it was not the original, and took a picture of Paul, Lib, and John in front of it."

I sensed a new closeness to Samuel Clemens and a new apprecia-tion of his wit. His own life story provided as much intrigue and pathos as the characters in his books. Sam's father died when Sam was eleven. Sam was apprenticed to a printer and subsequently had many adventures. He lived many places, including Europe. At age 70, he said the way to reach that age was to "have a scheme that would kill everybody else," meaning to go full speed at what you do.

Visiting Mark Twain's boyhood home was like getting in touch with my own soul. I was beginning to realize the depths of my own passion to write. By touching, even from a distance in time, the life of Samuel Clemens, I made a connection with a soulmate—not that I would ever achieve his creativity with words. But the passion was there and I was recognizing it, which meant I was being true to myself.

The four of us walked back to the car and subsequently John drove us to our motorhomes at the Steamboat Bend Shopping Center. In no time, John and Lib had driven the tow car up close to the rear of their motorhome and John hitched the two vehicles together.

As I settled into the passenger seat of our motorhome and saw the campground directory lying on the floor within easy reach, I recalled that there were several campgrounds from which to choose for that night in the Springfield area, but the next night (Thursday) we would be somewhere in Ohio along I-70. I remembered that on a previous trip, Paul and I had found a scarcity of campgrounds close to the highway along that interstate. Even John knew we might have some difficulty finding a campground close to where we wanted to stop the next night. Sometimes we have had to either stop earlier in the day than we had planned or drive later that we had hoped in order to find a campground not too far off our travel route. We usually take such circumstances in stride, counting them as part of the adventure of RV travel.

The campground directory would guide our decision. That "bible" offered state maps with campground locations as well as written descriptions, including directions on how to find a specific campground and ratings for completeness of facilities, cleanliness of rest rooms, and visual appeal.

John came on the CB to see if we were in communication and if we were ready to continue our day's travel. We were all set to go.

16

Outrunning a Storm

AT 10:55 A.M. on that Wednesday, June 7, we drove away from the Steamboat Bend Shopping Center, leaving the Mark Twain historic site behind us. We soon crossed the Mississippi River, the border between Missouri and Illinois. Paul and I looked at the bounteous, moving, muddy water. Just as the river's free-spirited water moved along on its way south to St. Louis (where we had crossed it on the way out to Colorado) and the Gulf of Mexico, so we moved on U.S. 36/I-72 toward Springfield, Illinois. I was still thinking about where we would camp when we got to Ohio the next evening.

"So long, another state, Missouri," said John over the CB.

"One more memory!" replied Paul.

Our duo-caravan progressed steadily ahead and crossed the Illinois River.

"Illinois River has been out of its banks also," John said on the CB.

"I would very much say so," Paul agreed. Trees stood like patient elephants in muddy water beside the main trough of the river.

As noon and lunchtime neared, John said over the CB, "We've got an exit up here a mile. I think we'll just get off and see where we can park it."

"That's all right. No problem," said Paul.

As we approached the exit, John took a quick survey of the area and said, "Well, I changed my mind. Doesn't look like a place to park."

"Yeah, and no place to turn around. We're used to eating on the fly. Do whatever you want to do," said Paul.

No rest areas were provided along that section of I-72. The nearest one was closer to Springfield, an hour and a half away.

Rather than parking on the shoulder of I-72, John decided to try an exit that led to Winchester, Illinois, three miles or so off the interstate highway. At the north edge of Winchester, he spotted a drive-in restaurant that was closed (out of business, actually) with a large paved area in front of it. We parked the motorhomes safely in its unused exit driveway. As we ate lunch under cloudy skies, we watched truck and car traffic go into and out of Winchester.

By 1:35 P.M., John and Paul registered at Mr. Lincoln's Campground, 3045 Stanton Avenue, Springfield, Illinois. There was also a Mr. Lincoln's RV Center on the premises, reportedly the largest RV parts and accessories store in the area.

Almost immediately after arriving at the campground, John and Lib unhooked the tow car and John drove it as we looked for a mall. We found White Oaks Mall in Springfield. A Regis Salon stylist shampooed and blow-dried my hair while Lib, John, and Paul browsed in the mall.

Afterward, with the help of the campground's free map and the AAA TourBook® guide, we found the parking lot for the Lincoln

Home Visitor Center in downtown Springfield. Inside, we received free tickets for the Lincoln Home National Historic Site tour. We were instructed to join the park ranger in front of the Lincoln Home ten minutes before the 3:45 P.M. tour time stamped on the ticket.

The handsome, two-story, elegantly restored home was on a broad, shady street at 8th and Jackson Streets. It is the only home that Lincoln ever owned. The house was built in 1839. Lincoln bought it in 1844 and lived there with his family for 17 years.

On one side of our tour ticket was a photograph of the home as it appeared in 1860. It was identical to what we saw that afternoon except that the house in the photograph looked like it could have used some fresh paint.

While we waited for our tour to begin near the Lincoln house with a small group of other people, John and Lib read the "Lincoln Home" brochure that we had picked up at the visitor center. After a group of tourists poured out of the historic home and down its front steps onto the brick pavement, it was our turn. Soon we stepped into the foyer and then into the various rooms. The park ranger described

"The handsome, two-story, elegantly restored home was on a broad, shady street at 8th and Jackson Streets. It is the only home that Lincoln ever owned." [Foreground: the author]

each room, the furniture, and the activities of Abraham Lincoln and his family.

I was surprised to learn that Lincoln was 6 feet 4 inches tall, wore a size 14 shoe, and never grew a beard until he went to Washington as president-elect. His wife, Mary, was only 5 feet 2 inches tall and wore a size 5 shoe.

As I walked up the stairs to the bedrooms, I reminded myself that President Abraham Lincoln, Honest Abe, a man and a legend, had stepped on those very treads. How awesome!

To bring myself down to earth, I walked outside to the rear of the backyard to see the interior of the privy. It was a three-seater with individual wood-slatted stools rather than one board with three holes laid across the privy bench.

I don't know if it was the aura of honesty around Abe Lincoln, but I sensed integrity as I walked the restored historic area near the Lincoln Home. The mostly two-story, Victorian houses in the neighborhood looked neat, ample, well kept, and unpretentious yet digni-

"To bring myself down to earth, I walked outside to the rear of the backyard [of the Lincoln Home] to see the interior of the privy. It was a three-seater with individual wood-slatted stools rather than one board with three holes laid across the privy bench."

fied. Seeing the area transported me back to the 1800s to a time of laborious tasks such as beating rugs and time-consuming travel by horse and train. Yet it was an era with time to think, time to recognize blessings, time to feel tragedy, time to heal. I forced myself to think of the problems the people of those days faced compared with those that we face—slavery for them, racism for us; gambling for them, drugs for us; assassination of the president for them, violence everywhere for us.

After leaving the Lincoln Home area, John parked the car on another street. While he and Paul waited, Lib and I walked to the Dana-Thomas House built in 1902–1904. Designed by Frank Lloyd Wright, it was one of his revolutionary Prairie Houses. Rather than conforming to the Victorian style of his time, he created a style suited to the flat Midwestern landscape. It was too late in the afternoon to take a tour or to enter, but we marveled at the architectural details as we walked its front and side perimeter. How we would have loved to see the inside. Its exterior design reminded us partly of the Orient and partly of the Mediterranean. The house sprawled half a block, looking fresh, enduring, and contemporary even that day. As if creating a story, Mr. Wright, then a young architect from Chicago, brought fresh ideas to his design of that elaborate family home of Susan Lawrence Dana, a Springfield socialite.

On the way back to the campground, we stopped for dinner at a Bob Evans Restaurant. Then John kindly drove to an Eagle grocery store near the campground where Paul and I bought about $25 worth of groceries. Lib had only an item or two to buy. John read *USA Today* as he waited in the car for us. Lib promptly got her groceries and joined him in reading.

We had done everything we set out to do that day—Mark Twain, my hairdo, and Abe Lincoln—with dinner out and buying groceries besides.

The next day, Thursday, June 8, would be a full day of driving. We had only one place to look for on the way—an antiques auction building. At dinner the night before, John had talked about trying to find the building, which should be along our route. It would be just a matter of spotting it. In addition, we would be in Ohio by the end of the day and hoped to find a campground not too far off the interstate.

As I sat on the sofa in the motorhome, the morning sun came through the window behind me. Outside it was 60 degrees with a lively breeze. The shadow of my head lay on the chair arm and the wall opposite me. The laptop computer was balanced on my knees; my feet in tennis shoes were planted squarely on the rose and blue runner that lay along the length of the motorhome. Anticipating a warm, humid day, I wore a pale-flowered top with cap sleeves and white Bermuda shorts. Pearl earrings complemented the white button effect on my blouse, which hung loosely over my shorts.

Paul returned to our site from taking the trash to the dumpster. He opened our entry door and asked what time it was. Paul had not worn a wrist watch for years because the metal makes his skin break out in a rash.

"We're ready a half-hour ahead of time! Can you believe it?" I laughed.

"I think I'm just going to unhook the water and electricity and be done with it," Paul said.

"Okay."

Mr. Lincoln's Campground lived up to the connotation of its name—honest, full value, and wholesome. Although located in the city of Springfield, it was countrylike with lawns, medium-sized leafy trees, and picnic tables with attached seats. Some sites were empty. All was quiet except the birds and Paul moving about outside.

"Mosquitoes and gnats out there this morning," said Paul as he entered, taking off his green sweater.

"Did you see anything of John or Lib this morning?"

"No, not yet," he said.

"I went down to the office to look for a paper. Not any papers there."

"You mean they just aren't in yet or they don't have them?"

"They don't have a paper machine down there."

All in all, I liked Springfield. Its restored historic area with unpretentious but ample houses seemed a fitting place for Abe Lincoln to have lived, and our campground with its bird songs and tree-shaded sites made me reluctant to leave. Springfield gave me a renewed sense of the true morals and values that make our lives secure and peaceful.

As we left the campground at 7:38 A.M., John came on the CB, asking in CB lingo if Paul could hear him.

"Got a copy there, Milkweed?"

Paul replied that he copied. It was a check to be sure both CBs were on and working.

"Boy! It doesn't look good south and west. Maybe we can outrun 'em," John said, referring to dark clouds. A few sprinkles of rain showed on the windshield.

Before leaving Springfield, we stopped at a Shell station for gasoline for our motorhome. While Paul was pumping gasoline, Lib walked to our driver's window and volunteered to mail a card that I had written from the four of us to a friend back home. She had seen a mailbox in the adjacent shopping center. I had just taken my rain bonnet out of my pocketbook to make the same trek.

"It won't hurt *my* hair," smiled Lib as I handed her the card for which she and John provided the stamp. Lib was blessed with naturally wavy hair that she managed beautifully, whereas my hair was fine, straight, and required a permanent every three months to curl it. Windy, humid weather would undo my hair styling of the day before. Bless Lib! She and John drove to the adjacent shopping center parking lot, mailed the card, and waited for us there.

In fact, bless Lib and John for their fun and relaxed company the whole trip. They were two special people in their consideration and generous friendship—great hosts at home and abroad!

After the gas fill-up, the four of us regained I-72 and headed east to Decatur, Illinois. From there we would travel the bypass and go northeast to Champaign, Illinois, where we would pick up I-74 toward Indianapolis, Indiana. The sunshine that had warmed my back at the campground had disappeared. Clouds covered us.

We crossed the Sangamon River. It had overflowed its banks earlier, leaving water standing in nearby fields. Sweet-smelling honeysuckle bloomed among lush foliage on a bank beside the road.

I began listening to tapes from the Christian Writers Conference.

"Milkweed, did you hear the radio news? Violent thunderstorms about 40 miles west of Springfield, so we might be able to outrun them for a while," John said at 8:25 A.M. over the CB. "Radio said Macon's about to get clobbered right now. I think we can outrun them to the border." John added, "Sure looks black back to the west."

"I agree. If you want to roll a little faster, it's all right with me," Paul responded.

"If the storm's doing 30 and we do 50 or 55, we ought to stay a little ahead of it, for a while anyway," John computed. John and Paul both used logic, not emotion or panic, in any situation involving stormy weather.

I peered outside my passenger seat window and turned my head toward the rear of our motorhome. The sky looked as dark as night. In front of us, it was overcast but light.

Even though I was worried, I think I would have been even more nervous if Paul and I had been alone on that road. It eased my mind a little to hear Paul and John stay abreast of our situation over the CB.

So far on the trip, we and the Graybeals had traveled in tandem. When we stopped at rest areas, we parked side by side or one in front of the other, depending on the parking area design. We always stayed together on the highway and whenever we stopped for gasoline or to rest.

We usually used the tow car together with John driving. We ate out, did grocery shopping and mall shopping, got hairdos and nails done, and went sightseeing together. Only once did I stay in the motorhome while the other three went shopping (in Wheat Ridge, Colorado) and that was because I was trying to rest and recuperate from a cold at the time. Lib drove her car alone twice: once to exchange an item at a camping store and once to cross the bridge at Royal Gorge. We traveled in individual motorhomes but stayed together as a foursome in sightseeing and other activities.

At that moment, I appreciated their company on the road, even though they were 100 yards in front of us.

"The darkness is getting closer," I said as I looked behind us.

"I don't think we're outrunning it," Paul replied at 9:32 A.M. "Not totally, anyhow. Of course, we're only going the speed limit. The speed limit for motorhomes is 55 in Illinois," Paul added.

"If the storm's headed east and we're going northeast, the fact that we're going on an angle gives it an advantage," Paul reasoned. "I've been watching it and I still haven't seen any lightning," he observed as he looked back to his left.

I looked across the coach through Paul's window. Dark clouds had crept toward us from that side.

As the highway turned more directly east, the dark stormy sky receded on Paul's side and advanced on my side of the motorhome. So far no rain fell on us from the storm we were trying to outrun.

A batch of black-eyed Susans blinked at me from the roadside.

"That storm must be going more than 40 miles an hour. It's gaining on us," John's voice came over the CB.

"We're going on an angle," Paul said.

"Soon as we head toward Indianapolis, we'll be heading due east," John said, implying that we should leave the storm behind us at that point.

A little later Paul said to me, "It's catching up with us. It's really getting windy out there, I'll tell you that." The wind pushed against the coach. Still no rain fell on the windshield, but dark clouds moved directly overhead and to my right. Lightning flashed.

"Shoot. It's right over us," I said of the dark clouds. I saw that the street lights had come on as we passed a small town.

"We're going to get the storm here after a bit," Paul predicted.

"Tornado weather. No doubt about that. Could have one," Paul said to me a little while later. First an unexpected snowstorm in the Colorado mountains and now a possible tornado, I thought—neither had been in my itinerary!

A violent rain-and-hail storm scene from an earlier time flashed into my mind's eye. Paul and I had been traveling alone in our motorhome in the northwestern states. As we approached Great Falls, Montana, the sky ahead looked dark and foreboding. By the time we drove into the storm, we had already passed the only place to pull off the road and the shoulder was too narrow to be a safe haven. We had to keep moving slowly ahead to avoid a rear-end collision from traffic behind us. The strong winds felt as if they would overturn our vehicle. Sheets of rain mixed with pellets of hail drenched the windshield and bombarded the coach. Paul could see only a foot or two ahead. I prayed for help and safety as we crept along, our flasher lights warning others of our slow speed. The storm passed over us as we drove through it. My prayers for safety were answered. As we entered Great Falls, we saw the storm's devastation—downed power lines, broken tree limbs on the ground, uprooted trees, and streets that had been blocked off because of the storm's damage. Since that time, I had not taken lightly any signs of foul weather such as the dark clouds looming behind us.

"He's picked up his speed five miles an hour, too," smiled Paul, referring to John. "He's running almost 65."

All of the trucks and cars on the road drove with their headlights turned on. Straight ahead the eastern sky looked light, but dark clouds coming from the west advanced toward it.

"He's backed off a little bit now," Paul said of John, who had reduced his speed to around 60.

"Looks like that wind is stirring up dust in the field, isn't it?" Paul asked John on the CB.

"It is," John replied.

"We might be making a little bit of headway now. I think you helped the total situation back there when you stepped up to 65."

"I didn't realize I was going that fast. With the tail wind, it just picked up on me," John noted.

I asked Paul, "Is it hard to steer?"

"No, no."

"I think we may be gaining on it a little," I said, noticing the dark cloud had receded from the overhead view in front of us. While a dark arch of clouds hovered over us, the sky ahead grew brighter and the light area grew wider. The anxious pressure of the storm lessened within me.

At 10:37 A.M. a sign welcomed us to Indiana.

"Well, do you think we've outrun the storm?" I asked Paul.

"We're ahead of it at the moment, more so than we were. Yeah." Paul cautiously conceded.

A sign said 76 miles to Indianapolis. I put on my sunglasses because of the glare from the cloudy but bright sky ahead. The storm's darkness was receding.

At 11:00 we pulled briefly into a rest area off of I-74 near mile marker 22.

John walked back to our coach. He stood outside Paul's window while they discussed a plan to take Route 32 to I-65 north of Indianapolis and then stop at a rest area on I-70 east of Indianapolis for lunch. We hoped we could stay ahead of the storm by delaying lunch and moving on at that point. We would eat a snack inside our rigs as we rode on the highway. That capability was just one daily comfort that we enjoyed about our motorhome.

Paul went to the rest room (another convenience of motorhomes) and then said he would like some graham crackers as he got back behind the wheel. As I got the box from the pantry rolling shelf, I heard Paul tell John on the CB that he was ready whenever they were.

Almost immediately we moved forward. I took the box of graham crackers to Paul, fishing one out for him and leaving the open box handy under the television pedestal on his side.

"Boy, just that short of a stop and the storm is getting ahead of us. Just four minutes," I said to Paul. Dark clouds now once again preceded us, arching overhead. There was no rain yet. Indianapolis was 46 miles ahead.

We exited I-74 onto the two-lane Route 32. It was busy with trucks and under construction as a shoulder was being installed on the right-hand side of the road. No dark clouds appeared in any direction. Paul said, "The storm seems to have dissipated."

Instead of waiting longer for lunch, our twosome caravan pulled into the parking lot at the rear of Lee's Inn in Lebanon. We had outrun the storm that chased us all morning! We came through with no rain, only wind.

After lunch in our coaches, we soon made our way to the six-lane I-65, traveled around the north side of Indianapolis, and continued east on I-70. The storm excitement during the morning had kept me too busy to think about where we would camp that night in Ohio. By 3:10 P.M. we entered Ohio, which meant we had a comfortable amount of time to find a campground near I-70 before it got dark.

An hour later we turned off I-70 at exit 47 and registered at nearby Enon Beach Campground, Springfield, Ohio. From having camped there on one of Paul's and my earlier trips, I recognized its office and nearby lake with a tall, white, lifeguard chair on the beach. I noted that the night before we had camped at a different Springfield—in Illinois.

How grateful we were to have outrun the violent, threatening storm that day. That afternoon, the sun shone, although the sky was mostly cloudy.

After we found and parked in our assigned sites, Libby walked next door to our coach. Seeing her approach, I stepped outside to meet her. She asked if we wanted to eat in or out. She said John had to unhook the tow car in any event in order to pull out of the site in the morning. I asked Paul what he wanted to do; he said either way was fine with him, and the same was true for me.

"Do *you* want to eat out?" I asked Lib.

"Oh, sure!" she laughed. That settled it. As we rode into town, we passed a billboard advertising Stocksdale's Family Restaurant and decided to head for it. With all of us chiming in with directions to John, we found the restaurant and a parking place close to the building.

After taking a number and waiting about 10 minutes, we followed the host to the very back of the second dining room and scrambled into a vinyl-covered booth. Soon we were eating generous portions of food and talking about our day on the road.

John and Lib kidded me about writing a book about our trip, wondering if they could get a copy wholesale. We had not talked about what would happen to my notes except that John had asked for a copy of them when I made a printout for myself. I hoped to put all my notes into the computer at home, edit them, and give a copy to John and Lib. I also planned to include photographs at appropriate places. When I was done, Paul and I would take the Graybeals to a nice restaurant and give them a custom-made album of the trip. I knew that when I got home a lot of things would need to be done, but I wanted very much to give that project first priority. My notes might also lead to an article and a short story or two, maybe even a book.

Before going back to our motorhomes from the restaurant, John drove the car in the same direction we would go the next morning to be sure of the route. It was only a short distance and we soon returned to the campground.

"What time tomorrow, John?" I asked.

This was our usual question by now. Thinking through the distance to go and stops to make, John said he thought eight o'clock ought to be about right. We all agreed.

"Now let me be sure I have the same time as you. What time do you have?" I asked John. My watch agreed with his.

It was still daylight when Paul and I said good night to John and Lib, then went to our motorhome a few steps away.

Inside, Paul relaxed by reading the newspaper and watching television. I tallied the trip log, took my usual daily shower, and relaxed in the living room with Paul. Our motorhomes had traveled 353 miles that day. We were about one-fourth of the way across Ohio. It was too soon to be certain about when we would arrive home in Maryland.

17

"Adios and All of That"

PAUL TURNED ON THE TELEVISION
about seven o'clock on that cloudy Friday morning, June 9, at Enon
Beach Campground near Springfield, Ohio. As I ate breakfast, I wondered if that day would be our last full day on the road before reaching our homes in Maryland. If we drove most of the day, we could
arrive home on Saturday. We were in western Ohio and had not yet
seen the antique mall that the Graybeals hoped to visit. The Fostoria
Outlet, somewhere in Ohio as I remembered, held my interest if it
were near our homeward route.

Our motorhome was parked beside the shimmering water of Enon
Lake. On the beach stood a solitary, vacant, tall, white, lifeguard
lookout chair. It was a cool morning, about 60 degrees outside.

Paul came in from unhooking the electricity.

"Okay. I'm going to get down off these jacks and get ready to go dump," he said, referring to the hydraulic levelers under the motorhome chassis.

Soon we drove slowly on a perimeter campground road, passing tenters and permanent campers until we saw the dump station. Earlier that morning, Paul had looked at the campground diagram he received during registration the day before, then he had walked the campground roads to locate the dump station.

I sat in the front passenger seat with the computer on my lap while Paul dumped the contents of the gray and black water holding tanks into the campground sewer's concrete opening. Just beyond a mixture of deciduous and pine trees on my right, I saw and heard traffic rushing along the interstate.

On my left, a robin, then another, landed on the seat of a rustic red picnic table, hopped along briskly on it, and flew away. A squirrel soon jumped up on the bench at the table, ran across its length, leaped down, then ran across the road in front of me and into the brush at the roadside. A mourning dove, then another, scouted the road and grass, pecking and jerking as they walked, then flew off.

I saw no people moving about. All of the trailers sat nestled in their sites, inanimate, yet I thought the people inside must be friendly toward their environment or else the birds and squirrels would not appear as freely as they did.

Paul finished dumping and we drove to the location where the Graybeals waited to leave the campground.

"Milkweed, do you have a copy?" John said on the CB when he saw our motorhome approach.

"Yeah. Let's get out of here. The mosquitoes are giving me a fit!" Paul said.

"Lib says that's what happens when you're sweet. Nothing bit her," John said jokingly.

During his brief interlude outdoors, Paul had received numerous bites and showed me one just under his glasses on his face. Another swollen bite protruded from the corner of his upper lip. He also had one on his cheek, one on his neck, three on one leg, and two on the other. He asked me to get the After Bite®, an effective treatment for insect bites and stings that we had learned about from our wagonmasters on our earlier trip to Alaska. After saving what I had just typed in the laptop computer, I gave him several applications of the clear liquid on his finger, which he then applied to the itching mosquito bites.

It was about eight o'clock when we left the campground. Even as we rode along on I-70, Paul found more mosquito bites that needed treatment.

Along with other cars and trucks, we turned on our headlights in the morning haze. Paul and I hoped to treat John and Lib to their main meal that day, whenever and wherever that occurred. They had been such great traveling friends that hosting them to a meal could only be a *symbol* of our appreciation.

Paul wore his royal blue Alaskan cap, his cranberry short-sleeved knit shirt, navy Bermuda shorts, and black loafers. I sported tennis shoes, flowered Bermuda shorts with a white background, a red short-sleeved top, red earrings, and a red sweater.

That Friday morning, I rode along catching up on my computer journal before listening to tapes.

Shortly before 11:00, John announced on the CB, "Milkweed. Sign says 'Fostoria Outlet,' 5 miles ahead."

"Oh, great!" I raised up from my reclined passenger seat and looked to the right in time to see the Fostoria sign. I had been listening to a tape.

"All right. That perked up my navigator," Paul said.

"It perked up my cruise control," John added.

"Sorry to hear that." Paul knew it meant that the Pinnacle's cruise control was malfunctioning when John talked on the CB.

And so during that late Friday morning, the four of us browsed through the Fostoria Outlet at Cambridge, Ohio. It carried various patterns and pieces of Fostoria glassware and crystal at discounted prices, as well as other items such as flower arrangement accessories and candles.

We spotted a Cracker Barrel Old Country Store® within walking distance, so we decided to eat there. Paul and I hosted Lib and John because it would be our main meal for the day.

During lunch, John began talking with a woman at the next table only a few inches away. When she learned that we were from Maryland, she said enthusiastically that she and her husband were from Hancock, Maryland, and that her sister lived in Keymar, which is near our homes. We learned her maiden name and her married name; that she and her husband had daughters in Cincinnati, Ohio, and in Pennsauken, New Jersey; and that they were going by car to Cincinnati where that daughter would graduate the next day. It is fun to meet other travelers and discover your connections with one another. Our waiter was offering dessert before we knew it.

Too full from pecan pancakes and country ham (John, Lib, and me) and chicken and dumplings (Paul), we all declined dessert. Paul left a generous tip and paid the bill.

In the gift shop at the Cracker Barrel Old Country Store®, John bought a baseball cap that said "Antique Golfer. Been there, done that. Out golfing." He loves golf, and in my mind the "antique" part referred to his love for antiques.

Once again, as we had done on the way west, we took the detour from I-70 in Ohio onto U.S. 40. At the end of the detour, a mile of traffic was backed up on I-70 waiting to enter the detour area. They were heading west, we were traveling east.

The hazy, muggy weather had continued since our morning departure from the campground. I-70 took us across the Ohio River to Wheeling, West Virginia (we used the I-470 bypass); across that state's narrow, northern panhandle; and into Pennsylvania. John gave up looking for the antique mall. He had thought it was in Ohio; it may have been in the area of I-70 that we missed because of the detour. I hoped that our stops at the Antique Mall on the way out in Springfield, Ohio; the antique stores in Cripple Creek, Colorado; and the Rocky Mountain Antiques mall on the way back from Estes Park to Denver helped to ameliorate his disappointment.

At Washington, Pennsylvania, after about a 40-minute delay in traffic backed up on I-70, we maneuvered our way through road construction. By the time we reached the end of the construction area, two trucks and two cars occupied the space between the Graybeals and us. When we drove onto the dual lanes, the distance between us soon cleared and we once again saw the full word "Pinnacle" and the Graybeals' tow car.

Purple crown vetch bloomed on the roadsides and in the median strip of the dual highway of I-70. I continued listening to tapes about writing and jotting notes into my spiral tablet.

"Hottest my engine has registered since I left home," John said over the CB.

"Same with ours. It's probably because the outside temperature is the hottest since we left home," Paul said as we reached the brow of a hill.

On our trip, John had suggested campgrounds for our overnight stays. As a former designer, owner, and operator of Camp Safari near Williamsport, Maryland; a member of the Campground Owners Association; a safety inspector for a campground insurance company; and an inveterate motorhome traveler, he knew more than most travelers about campground locations. While we did not want to take undue advantage of him, we gladly received his suggestions both of how many miles to drive daily and where to camp.

Not wanting to be a strain on John's goodwill, however, I made every effort to do my own research in *Trailer Life Directory for Campgrounds, RV Parks & Services* and on maps, just as if Paul and I were traveling alone. Usually in the lead as we traveled, both John and Lib quickly perceived problems, found road signs, and pointed out interesting sights. They gave information and suggestions in logical, down-to-earth speech. They patiently repeated when asked and goodnaturedly brightened our conversations and times together.

Paul and I rode along behind John and Lib, not knowing where John might be planning to stay that Friday night but not being concerned about it. Paul talked about Friendship Village Campground and RV Park at Bedford, Pennsylvania. John also mentioned a campground near Connellsville, Pennsylvania.

John came on the CB again to say that we would head for Friendship Village Campground. He also said that our estimated time of arrival was 5:30 that evening per his navigator, Lib. John asked if Paul wanted to get gas before we entered the Pennsylvania Turnpike (I-76). Paul thought aloud about the number of miles to the campground and the amount of gasoline in the motorhome tank.

"Thirty-one [miles] to Staunton and about 70 after that," John calculated the mileage.

"I should be able to do that. Let's try it," Paul decided.

"Another deer on the right. Horrific! Somebody must be hitting them at night," John said. On the right lay the sixth lifeless deer we had seen that day. That one had a black wounded area at its shoulders.

"Chainsaw, my navigator is wondering if you want us to check Friendship Village to see if they have room for us," Paul asked John on the CB.

"Yes, if you want to do that. I expect they would have room for us," returned John.

"As soon as she finishes writing what she's writing, we'll see what we can do about that," Paul said.

Putting aside the spiral tablet, I looked up the campground number in the *Trailer Life* directory and called on the cellular telephone, using the 800 number listed. The call went through right away. I reserved two pull-through sites with 30-ampere electric service, side by side. It was a comfort to know the reservations would hold two sites for us at the beginning of what might be a busy weekend.

I picked up the spiral tablet again. While I had not hidden my note taking and journal writing, I had not made a show of it, preferring to keep it low key. I wasn't sure what I would do with all my notes, but something inside me cried out to log the trip. I had tried not to let it interfere with talking with Paul as we rode together in the motorhome or to let it affect my relationship with Lib and John.

After all, this was their vacation, too, so I did not want to impose my writing on them when I was supposed to be having fun with them. Paul supported my note taking and computer writing, commenting on it in positive ways to Lib and John. I did not sense any restraint on Lib and John's part because they knew I was taking notes. In fact, they seemed to enjoy it, as when John said maybe I had in my notes how many sunny days we had had to that point. And they both wanted to read my "book" of our trip.

We crossed the Monongahela River. It looked normal, not muddy like the rivers in the Midwest. Nor was the Youghiogheny River grimy. By then, we had counted eight deer lying along the road, apparently hit by vehicles.

At almost four o'clock, Paul reached out his window for a ticket from the tollbooth at New Staunton as we entered the Pennsylvania Turnpike. Along that dual highway, many locust trees bloomed. The Pennsylvania mountains looked like giant heads of broccoli with their leafy, dense growths of deciduous trees. I tried to compare them to the Colorado Rocky Mountains—snowcapped with jagged boulders, striated colors, and deep gorges—but I couldn't because they are so different.

"We've outrun showers all the way from Colorado. Looks like we may catch up with one," John said. Dark shadows appeared ahead and to the right.

"Lib wanted to get her car washed, maybe this will do it for her," added John. I strained to hear the last part correctly as the CB sound dwindled.

The sky looked ominous. Tree branches barely moved—strange. I looked at my watch. The digital seconds blinked up at me. I held my breath as if something either dire or awesome was about to happen. It was that eerie calm before the storm. I wondered if we would get to the campground before the rain started. I was glad I had made reservations by telephone earlier that afternoon.

A dark cloud hung heavily above us, and the sky looked hazy ahead as it had all day. No rain came. That made me breathe easier. When I looked over at Paul, my apprehensions suddenly subsided. "I just saw where you put your money," I laughed as I looked at the folded $5 bill tucked between the side frame of his glasses and his right ear. He was ready to pay the turnpike toll.

We emerged from the well-lit, two-lane Allegheny Mountain Tunnel in haze but no rain and no dark clouds. We moved on toward Bedford, about 20 miles ahead.

"Well, I believe I see a little sunshine. Even see a little blue sky up there. Well. That's nice," I said to Paul as we neared the Bedford tollbooth to exit the Pennsylvania Turnpike.

Ten minutes later, at 5:33 P.M. (a great time estimation by Lib!), we drove into Friendship Village Campground and RV Park, Bedford, Pennsylvania, in sunshine. Paul and John registered our motorhomes for the last time that trip. The next day would take us home.

After 345 miles that day, Paul and I were ready to settle in for the evening. At the moment, he was outside connecting our RV to the campground utilities.

"We drove into Friendship Village Campground and RV Park, Bedford, Pennsylvania, in sunshine. Paul and John registered our motorhomes for the last time . . . The large, shady campground was serene." [L-R: the Beards' motorhome and the Graybeals' motorhome.]

Lib came to the dinette window that I had just opened. "Do you want to go antiquing with us or are you going to party poop?" Lib laughingly said to me after she had already gotten a decline from Paul.

"I think I'd better party poop with Paul. You two can do your antique antics," I said, laughing.

During the trip, each of us looked out for and included the other, both individually and as couples. Like the Three Musketeers, we were all for one and one for all. When we saw free brochures, Lib and I had picked them up for one another. When the Graybeals wanted to go antiquing, they invited us also. That evening at the campground was no exception.

The Graybeals left the campground in the tow car to go antiquing. Paul hooked up to electricity and water and leveled the coach. The large, shady campground was serene. Paul and I each prepared our own supper, getting whatever we wanted to eat, having had our main meal at noon at the Cracker Barrel Old Country Store®.

John and Lib returned in about fifteen minutes. The antique place was closed.

After trying to watch the evening news on our television, which was not getting good reception that evening, Paul and I walked next door to discuss the next day's departure time with Lib and John.

"Bernice would like to get home in time to pick up our mail at the post office," Paul said.

"What time does that close?" John asked.

"Either 12:00 or one, I'm not sure which, but I think 12 on a Saturday," I said.

"I want to get home to do my laundry," Lib said. Then she jokingly added that she thought John would lose no time in getting to the golf course.

"I play in a tournament Tuesday," John grinned.

After mentally calculating the distance, John suggested 7:30, asking Lib if that was okay with her since she is not a morning person.

"Sure," said Lib as she showed me the beautifully smocked dresses that she had been crafting at odd moments on the trip. She was making them for children of friends. Her work was detailed and exquisite.

"I would like to get a picture of the four of us and our motorhomes when we have a rest stop tomorrow," I said.

We all decided to stop at South Mountain Rest Area for the photograph. Surely someone else would be there to snap the picture.

After more conversation and saying it had been another good day, Paul and I said good night, although it was daylight, and returned next door to our motorhome.

Back inside, it seemed strange to write in my spiral tablet on an unmoving dinette table. I must say, I hadn't realized how readable my handwriting could be.

Paul read *USA Today*, then got out some of his motorhome record books to see when the oil and other filters would need changing, tasks he would do at home. Meanwhile, I wrote in my tablet and listened to writing tapes.

When I awoke on Saturday morning, I could hardly believe that it would be our last day on the road—already!

After dressing and eating our usual breakfasts in the motorhome, we began to prepare for unloading the coach once we got home. Doing as much as possible before we got home made the unloading there go quickly and smoothly. I reminded myself that out of sight is out of mind and that I must open doors and drawers to be sure all went into the house that should.

Paul helped to put clean sheets on the bed. Then I began stuffing plastic grocery bags with newspapers and trip brochures collected en route, cosmetics, audio tapes, shoes, bath towels and dish towels, and whatever needed stowing in a bag to take into the house when we got home. I put the Bible in my briefcase and the laundry into a huge, black plastic bag. I left intact the food and clothes drawers until we got home so their contents would be easily available en route as needed.

The filled plastic bags were stashed out of our way, back in the bedroom on my side, on the sofa, beside the computer cabinet, in the shower tub, and on the forward dinette seat. (Items are less likely to fall off the forward dinette seat because the back of the seat serves as a barrier should we stop quickly.)

As I moved about, I heard Lib laughing outside the dinette window. Usually she was not outside the motorhome before we left a campground. She walked over to our dinette window, which I slid open. "Would you say that again?" I asked.

"Greater love hath no one than getting up early on a Saturday morning!" she exclaimed, holding a cup of coffee in both hands. We both laughed heartily. A night person, she loved to sleep late.

"Wait! Let me take your picture," I said, and I hurried outside.

As our motorhomes moved on the country lane of Friendship Village Campground and RV Park, Bedford, Pennsylvania, about 7:30 that Saturday morning, I said to Paul, "June 10th, dear, June 10th. Headed home."

A few minutes later, we stopped for gas at a service station; it was closed.

"They don't like to get up early on Saturday morning either," I said after seeing a sign on the office door stating that Monday through Friday the station opened at 7:00 A.M., but Saturday it opened at 8:00 A.M.

A little farther on, however, Paul filled the motorhome with gasoline at a convenience store. John and Lib waited in their motorhome; they did not need a refill that time since their vehicle gets more miles to the gallon than ours does.

It was another hazy, cloudy, overcast morning. As we turned onto I-70 East at Breezewood, a sign indicated that Washington, D.C. was 127 miles away and Baltimore, Maryland, 129 miles.

My mind raced at the thought of getting home—seeing Jeff and Nancy, looking through the mail, talking with friends, getting back to my computer, planning for new office equipment, writing and editing the story of our Colorado trip, inviting John and Lib to a restaurant meal to receive the story, listening to the writers conference tapes again, and generally getting on with my relationships and hopes.

I thought of how I had changed during the trip to Colorado. Normally inclined to lead with my own ideas, I had become more likely to wait to see what other people wanted to do. I became more patient and respectful of other people's abilities to plan a route or choose a place to stay, less anxious to know the answer as soon as a question came into my mind. I had gotten into a vacation mode wherein someone else leads.

Traveling in Colorado opened my heart to its spectacular beauty, as well as the friendliness and warmth of its residents. I felt close to Coloradans, as if they could be my next-door neighbors instead of unknown people on the other side of the country.

I had come to know Lib and John better and to relax with them. Their consistent good humor and excellent hosting served as a model for me. I need have had no concern at the outset about what it would be like traveling together with friends on a long trip. We all got along well and our friendship deepened. What exciting memories we share! I was and would continue to be very thankful to John and Lib for inviting us to join them on the Colorado adventure. Like the Alaskan adventure, the Colorado journey had captured my heart.

Paul had impressed me, too. He had driven our motorhome all the way. He had joined in all the activities with good spirit and a positive attitude and, as usual at home, had considered me in what we did. His tactful good humor made us laugh. His knowledge of how things work both helped and impressed us, such as when John's cruise control fluctuated as he spoke on his CB.

My mind had been refreshed by all the new sights and adventures. At home it had felt dull and stifled. Now it felt alert and renewed.

I had new memories, new subjects to talk about, new inspiration, and a sense of having had a fulfilling vacation. Seeing the presidential centers as well as the Rockies was a good mix, one that spoke to my mind and eye.

I had changed spiritually. I learned to know that God blessed me even though I did not recognize his blessings most times. I learned through reading *An Introduction to Christian Writing* by Ethel Herr that consistent Bible study and prayer bring depth to one's beliefs. And I had read my Bible and prayed every morning on the trip. It was a discipline that I knew would help me in my relationships with God, Jesus, and the Holy Spirit as well as in my everyday life—learning, writing, personal interactions.

While I do so at home, I was surprised at how easy it was for me on the road to set the alarm for two hours before our departure time each day, get up, dress, pray a morning prayer, eat breakfast, and read the Bible. It showed the value of habit, that a good habit perpetuates itself, just as a bad one does.

We rode along I-70 toward Frederick. The Graybeals' Pinnacle and Honda rear lights led us homeward that morning. Morning mist and haze shrouded the scene ahead. Nearby, green foliage looked lush and damp. Purple crown vetch graced some of the roadsides.

At 9:30 we pulled into the rest area on South Mountain for the planned photo session. Sure enough, a kind man who was sweeping the area took three pictures of us. John learned that the man had a son who had attended a National Youth Conference of the Church of the Brethren held at Fort Collins, Colorado.

With hugs and thanks all around, the four of us realized that that was our last time together.

John said, "We'll take you to your exit and after that you're on your own!"

Laughing, we returned to our motorhomes and continued toward Frederick.

On the other side of Frederick, toward Walkersville, Paul said, "Corn looks good." Young green plants stood a foot high in a roadside field.

Farther on, a wheat field had already been harvested. The farm crops in Maryland were ahead of those in the Midwest.

At 10:30, we saw a sign: "Welcome to Carroll County." We were almost home.

We drove through Taneytown.

"We pulled into the rest area on South Mountain for the planned photo session. Sure enough, a kind man who was sweeping the area took three pictures of us." [L-R: Paul, the author, Lib, and John]

"Last lap," I said.

"For us," Paul noted.

"Yep."

"Well, we ought to be home by . . . what, 11?"

"Yeah, we should be." We turned at the Taneytown blinker light (since replaced by a traffic circle) onto Route 140 toward Westminster.

As we neared our turnoff from the Graybeals, who would go on to their home near Manchester, Paul said on the CB, "I think I can handle it from here. We do thank you. Adios and all of that."

"I've done about all I can do for you. We'll catch you on the rebound," John said.

"Thanks again. Thanks very much," Paul returned earnestly.

On our own, we rode up the long hill of our country road. Then Paul backed into our driveway at home. It was 10:54 A.M. Paul had driven all the way, 4,343 miles.

In the days that followed, I tallied the trip log:

Total miles:	4,343
Total days:	25
Average miles per day:	174
Total spent (including gasoline):	$2,107.32
Average spent per day:	$84.29
Average spent per day for campsites:	$15.80
Total spent for gasoline:	$618.03
Total gallons of gasoline:	513.32
Average cost per gallon:	$1.20
Miles per gallon:	8.46

Studies show that traveling by RV is from one-third to three-fourths less expensive than going by car and staying in commercial lodging. Those figures have been true for us. In addition, when we travel we enjoy the advantages of hanging up our clothes instead of packing them into a suitcase, sleeping in our own bed at night, having the bathroom and refrigerator at hand as we travel, and of course being able to go on our own schedule—usually without reservations. Cooking and cleaning are like child's play in a motorhome. We feel that whatever we spend for RV traveling is money well spent because of the value received.

As for how the trip to Colorado compared with the one to Alaska, it was like comparing ice cream with fudge brownies. I loved them both. And they were both as captivating as luscious desserts. We had a heftier serving of Alaska because that trip was 44 days long compared with the 25-day trip to Colorado. But both trips more than met our expectations.

Their similarities stood out like the candles on Paul's birthday cake. Alaska offered the famous Mount McKinley, Colorado the equally famous Pikes Peak. In Alaska we traveled the exciting Top of the World Highway, toured historical museums, frolicked in the Liard hot springs, walked on the flat tundra of Barrow, and admired the beadwork of Athabascan Indians. In Colorado, we experienced the perilous Million Dollar Highway, visited the Denver Museum of Natural History, bobbed up and down in the Glenwood Springs hot springs, stood on the level mesa at Mesa Verde National Park, and admired the black sculptures of the Pueblo Indians.

Their differences were also notable. While Alaska offered polar bears and musk oxen, Colorado had ancient cliff dwellings. In Alaska we got fogged in at Barrow, drove our motorhomes onto a ferry at Skagway, and camped in the wilderness without utility hookups. In Colorado, we got stranded in snow, rode the narrow gauge railway to Silverton, and found utility hookups everywhere we traveled.

The rest of our lives would include cherished memories of that Colorado adventure. I would never again think of a trip to Colorado as dull and question whether it was worth taking. What did I learn? For the thousandth time, I learned not to assume—to let each trip have its own special place in my personal history.

Epilogue

MY COMPANIONS on the Colorado trip showed heroism. Voluntarily, Lib bravely drove the car alone across the world's highest suspension bridge over Royal Gorge in Colorado.

John held on during their snowy climb to Coal Bank Hill Pass summit under extremely hazardous driving conditions and continued to cope with a potentially dangerous drive on the Million Dollar Highway.

Paul remained calm and in charge during our snowstorm stranding and when driving over the perilous Million Dollar Highway. After the trip, I asked him if he had been scared when he was driving on the Million Dollar Highway. "Nope," he said. "I had confidence in the vehicle. I had decided if I lost my brakes, I was going to bank it regardless of any damage to the motorhome. I wasn't going to ride out the curves looking for the road to flatten out or get less steep or wait to find a runaway ramp. No, I wouldn't mind driving over that again." He meant that, if he had to, he would have driven the motorhome off the road into the side of the mountain on a slight angle to slow the coach down. He would not stay on the road without brakes going downhill because he might not be able to negotiate every curve without overturning the vehicle because of the growing speed.

The only grit I showed was to keep on sightseeing in spite of mountain sickness and a dripping, coughing cold. Later I learned from information on a Colorado map that at elevations above 5,000 feet, it is normal to notice a faster heartbeat and increased rate of breathing due to lower oxygen levels. For the first two or three days, some people may experience dizziness, fatigue, headaches, nasal congestion, and difficulty in sleeping. To adjust to the high altitudes, the map suggested that one, if possible, remain at 5,000 feet for a day or two before going higher; limit physical activity for the first few days; eat high-carbohydrate foods; ingest very little alcohol, caffeine, and salty foods; drink more than the usual amount of water; and have a positive, accepting attitude toward the altitude.

As for the snowstorm and our being stranded for two hours, it taught me to be realistic about such a possibility. I learned what being stranded in the elements is like and the loneliness, almost panic, that comes over one. Fortunately, we had a roof over our heads, food to eat, and a telephone to call for help. We are grateful our experience was short-lived, comparatively speaking.

Later at home, Paul said, "I'm sorry, dear, that the drive from Durango to Grand Junction made you feel so uncomfortable. As long as the roads were dry and clear, why, I thoroughly enjoyed it as the driver," and he chuckled. I thought how true that is for whoever drives. The driver has his or her attention on the road and feels in control whereas the passenger looks at hazards and may feel helpless to avoid them.

The weather took us by surprise. We could not believe we had so many rainy, misty, cool days. We enjoyed only four totally sunny days out of 25!

My mother-in-law used to say that she never let the weather keep her from doing what she wanted to do. That held true for us. For the most part, we went wherever our interests took us, no matter the weather. The exception was Pikes Peak, which ungraciously threw a snowstorm to keep us from its summit. However, we enjoyed a glorious, sunlit view of it from the distance as we left Colorado.

Because a kind of rhythm built up between him and John as they drove, Paul politely declined my offers to drive. In the end, he could say he drove all the way, all 4,343 miles. He did an excellent job!

Since our visit to the United States Air Force Academy gift store, the Mesa Verde National Park welcome center, and other gift shops in Colorado, I have often thought of my pen pal and how after all those years her simple gift had stirred my memory and given me a heartwarming connection with her Native American art of beautiful pottery making.

Far from being dull, the Colorado trip lit up our lives. When I asked Paul his thoughts about traveling with friends, he firmly and promptly stated, "I had no apprehensions and I thought it went well."

I need not have had any concern either about how the four of us would get along. We meshed all along the way, good humors and positive attitudes carrying each day. The trip together was fun and adventurous. We enjoy the company of Lib and John more than ever and hope they feel the same way.

I did come to some conclusions about traveling: If you go to Colorado in the springtime, you're going to have to cope with the weather—snow, floods, rain, hail, sleet, fog—and be cautious about traveling on wet or snowy mountain roads. Your body will also have to cope with the high altitudes. But you'll avoid the crowded tourist season.

Sir Winston Spencer Churchill (1874–1965) in a speech to the Canadian Senate and House of Commons, Ottawa (December 30, 1941), said it well:

> We have not journeyed all this way across the centuries, across the oceans, across the mountains, across the prairies, because we are made of sugar candy.

We didn't start out to prove what we were made of, but we were glad to discover we weren't made of sugar candy. The validation process, however, certainly thrust excitement into our travel.

In closing, thank you for coming along on this ride into springtime in the picturesque Rockies of Colorado. My best wishes to you as you travel on the road or by way of the written word.

Appendix

For additional information on motorhoming and traveling to Colorado, you may refer to the following sections in this appendix:

—Campground and Truck Center Directories
—Membership Benefit Cards
—The National Park System
—National Park System Sites in Colorado
—State Visitor Guides to Colorado
—Places of Renown Near Colorado
—Presidential Libraries and Museums
—Itinerary of Our Colorado Trip
—Campgrounds on Our Colorado Trip Itinerary
—Travel Checklist

Campground and Truck Center Directories

Paul and I keep on board our motorhome several campground and truck center directories. They are invaluable in finding a place to stay at night or a service center should it be needed. The list below includes some of the directories available in hard copy. In addition to those listed below, you may also check the Internet for campgrounds and RV services.

AAA Campbooks
Available to members only through local AAA offices. They include campgrounds in the United States and Canada.

Anderson's Campground Directory (for mid-Atlantic and southeast coastal regions)
P.O. Box 467
Lewisburg, WV 24901
888-645-1897; 304-645-1897
www.rvguide.com/andersons

Exit Authority®
Interstate America
5695-G Oakbrook Parkway
Norcross, GA 30093-9943
Orders: 800-494-5566

KOA Directory/Road Atlas/Camping Guide
Kampgrounds of America, Inc.
P.O. Box 30558
Billings, MT 59114-0558
(Free at any KOA campground in North America)
www.koakampgrounds.com

The RVer's Friend (lists diesel/gasoline locations and their camping services)
P.O. Box 476
Clearwater, FL 33757
Orders: 800-338-6317
www.truckstops.com

Trailer Life Directory for Campgrounds, RV Parks & Services
TL Enterprises Incorporated
2575 Vista Del Mar Drive
Ventura, CA 93001
800-234-3450; 805-667-4100
Fax 805-667-4454
www.camping.tl.com

Travel Centers & Truckstops
Interstate America
5695-G Oakbrook Parkway
Norcross, GA 30093-9943
Orders: 800-494-5566

Wheelers RV Resort & Campground Guide
Print Media Services, Ltd.
1310 Jarvis Avenue
Elk Grove Village, IL 60007
800-323-8899; 847-981-0100
Fax 847-981-0106

Woodall's Campground Directories (North American, Eastern, Western, Florida, Missouri/Kansas editions)
Woodall Publications Company
13975 West Polo Trail Drive
Lake Forest, IL 60045-5000
800-323-9076; 847-362-6700
Fax 847-362-8776
www.woodalls.com

Membership Benefit Cards

Certain clubs and organizations have arranged with participating campgrounds to offer discounts to RV travelers staying on their premises. Paul and I carry membership cards for AAA, Good Sam, and KOA. In addition we carry a Golden Age Passport for free admission to places in the National Park System. Further information about these cards is shown below. Other clubs and organizations also offer discounts or special membership prices at campgrounds.

- AAA. Members of this organization are eligible to receive discounts at participating campgrounds when they show their AAA membership cards. In addition, AAA offers its members free maps, trip routing, and invaluable TourBook® guides. Inquiries about joining may be made by checking a telephone directory for a local AAA office. Interested persons may also visit AAA's web site or write to the following address:

AAA
1000 AAA Drive
Heathrow, FL 32746-5063
www.aaa.com

- Good Sam RV Owners Club. This is the oldest and largest travel club for RVers. First-time membership dues are $30 for three years; thereafter, annual membership dues are $25. Membership benefits include a 10 percent courtesy discount at over 1,600 participating campgrounds and RV parks in the United States and Canada, 10 percent savings on RV parts and accessories at more than 1,000 service centers, 10 percent discount on LP gas, discounts on the *Trailer Life Directory for Campgrounds, RV Parks & Services,* free trip-routing service, free spouse membership, the *Highways* monthly magazine, and others. Persons may sign up at the club's web site or by writing to the following address:

Good Sam Club
64 Inverness Drive East
Englewood, CO 80122
800-765-6080
www.goodsamclub.com

- KOA. The KOA Value Kard® can be purchased for $10 at any KOA campground. It is good for two years and entitles its owners to a 10 percent discount at KOA Kampgrounds whether you pay by cash or credit card. It is also available by sending $10 and your name and address to:

Value Kard
P.O. Box 31734, Dept. D
Billings, MT 59107-1734
www.koakampgrounds.com

The National Park System

The National Park System (NPS) admits free to its parks those persons ages 16 and younger. Available at parks that charge entrance fees (most parks do charge a fee) are (1) the Golden Eagle Pass, which is a 12-month pass to all parks in the system; (2) a Golden Age Passport for United States citizens and permanent residents age 62 or older; and (3) a Golden Access Passport for qualifying persons with disabilities. None of the permits covers user, camping, or other fees. For additional information, contact the service at:

National Park System
Office of Public Inquiries
Room 1013
1849 C Street NW
Washington, D.C. 20240
202-208-4747
Business hours: 9 A.M.–12 noon; 1–4 P.M.
www.nps.gov

National Park System Sites in Colorado

Our National Park System is composed not only of forested parks such as the Rocky Mountain National Park but also specific sites such as the Florissant Fossil Beds National Monument (NM) and Bent's Old Fort National Historic Site (NHS). The National Park System includes the following sites in Colorado:

Bent's Old Fort NHS
35110 Highway 194 East
La Junta, CO 81050-9523
719-383-5010

Black Canyon of the Gunnison NM
102 Elk Creek
Gunnison, CO 81230-9304
970-249-1915

Colorado NM
Fruita, CO 81521-9530
970-858-3617

Curecanti National Recreation Area (NRA)
102 Elk Creek
Gunnison, CO 81230-9304
970-641-2337

Dinosaur NM
4545 E. Highway 40
Dinosaur, CO 81610-9724
970-374-3000

Florissant Fossil Beds NM
P.O. Box 185
Florissant, CO 80816-0185
719-748-3253

Great Sand Dunes NM
11500 Highway 150
Mosca, CO 81146-9798
719-378-2312

Hovenweep NM
McElmo Route
Cortez, CO 81321-8901
970-749-0510

Mesa Verde National Park (NP)
P.O. Box 8
Mesa Verde, CO 81300-0008
970-529-4465
Fax 970-529-4498
www.nps.gov/meve/

Rocky Mountain NP
Estes Park, CO 80517-8397
970-586-1206

State Visitor Guides to Colorado

For more information on what to see and do in Colorado, contact the following office for an Official State Vacation Guide that includes information on all seven regions of the state of Colorado:

Colorado Travel & Tourism Authority
P.O. Box 3524
Englewood, CO 80155
303-832-6171
800-265-6723
www.colorado.com

In addition, as you travel, welcome centers offer information and numerous materials for tourists.

Places of Renown Near Colorado

While there is a plethora of spectacular sights to see and activities to do in the state of Colorado itself, other famous marvels lie within a day's drive of Colorado's borders. Four of these well-known places in the National Park System are the following:

From Cortez or Durango in southern Colorado:

Petrified Forest NP
P.O. Box 2217
Petrified Forest National Park, AZ 86028-2217
520-524-6228

Grand Canyon NP
P.O. Box 129
Grand Canyon, AZ 86023-0129
520-638-7888

From Denver in northern Colorado:

Mount Rushmore National Memorial (N MEM)
P.O. Box 268
Keystone, SD 57751-0268
605-574-2523

Badlands NP
P.O. Box 6
Interior, SD 57750-9700
605-433-5361

Presidential Libraries and Museums

Presidential libraries and museums attract many visitors. There are 12 such historic sites across our country. Below is visitor information for these presidential libraries.

- George Bush Presidential Library and Museum
  1000 George Bush Drive West
  College Station, TX 77845
  409-260-9554
  Fax 409-260-9557
  E-mail: library@bush.nara.gov
  TTY 409-260-3770
  Open Monday through Saturday, 9:30 A.M.–5 P.M.; Sunday, 12 noon–5
    P.M., except Thanksgiving Day, Christmas Day, and New Year's Day
  Admission: Adults $3.00; students, senior citizens (62 and up), groups
    with reservations $2.50; children under 16, school groups, chaperones
    free

- Jimmy Carter Library
  441 Freedom Parkway
  Atlanta, GA 30307-1498
  404-331-3942
  Fax 404-730-2215
  E-mail: library@carter.nara.gov
  Open Monday through Saturday, 9:00 A.M.–4:45 P.M.; Sunday, 12
    noon–4:45 P.M., except New Year's Day, Thanksgiving Day, and
    Christmas Day
  Admission: Adults $5.00; over 55 $4.00; under 16 free

- Dwight D. Eisenhower Library
  200 S.E. 4th Street
  Abilene, KS 67410-2900
  785-263-4751
  Fax 785-263-4218
  E-mail: library@eisenhower.nara.gov
  Open daily, 9 A.M.–5:00 P.M., except Thanksgiving Day, Christmas Day, and New Year's Day. Beginning Memorial Day, open until 6:00 P.M. during the summer months
  Admission is free to all buildings except museum: Adults $3, over 61 $2.50, under 16 free

- Gerald R. Ford Library and Museum
  Library:
  1000 Beal Avenue
  Ann Arbor, MI 48109
  734-741-2218
  Fax 734-741-2341
  E-mail: library@fordlib.nara.gov
  Located on the Ann Arbor campus of the University of Michigan, the library is open Monday through Friday, 8:45 A.M.–4:45 P.M., except federal holidays
  Museum:
  303 Pearl Street NW
  Grand Rapids, MI 49504-5353
  616-451-9263
  Fax 616-451-9570
  E-mail: information.museum@fordmus.nara.gov
  The museum is open daily, 9:00 A.M.–4:45 P.M., except New Year's Day, Thanksgiving Day, and Christmas Day
  Admission: Adults $3, senior citizens $2, children under 15 free

- Rutherford B. Hayes Presidential Center
  Spiegel Grove
  Fremont, OH 43420-2796
  800-998-7737
  Fax 419-332-4952
  E-mail: hayeslib@rbhayes.com
  Open Monday through Saturday, 9 A.M.–5 P.M.; Sundays and holidays, 12 noon–5 P.M.

Admission to the home *or* museum: Adults $5.00, both home and museum $8.50; seniors (AAA/FT/CW Trust/NHS) $4.00, both $7.50; ages 6–12 $1.25, both $2.50; groups $4.00, both $7.50; school groups $.75, both $1.50; under age 6, OHS/HPC members free

- Herbert Hoover Presidential Library and Museum
  211 Parkside Drive
  P.O. Box 488
  West Branch, IA 52358-0488
  319-643-2541
  Fax 319-643-5825
  E-mail: library@hoover.nara.gov
  The library and museum are part of the 186-acre Herbert Hoover National Historic Site, which includes the Hoover Birthplace Cottage
  The museum is open daily, 9 A.M.–5 P.M., except Thanksgiving Day, Christmas Day, and New Year's Day
  Admission: Adults $2, senior citizens 62 and over $1, children under 16 free

- Lyndon Baines Johnson Library and Museum
  2313 Red River Street
  Austin, TX 78705-5702
  512-916-5137
  Fax 512-478-9104
  E-mail: library@johnson.nara.gov
  Open daily, 9:00 A.M.–5:00 P.M., except Christmas Day
  Admission: Free

- John Fitzgerald Kennedy Library and Museum
  Columbia Point
  Boston, MA 02125-3398
  617-929-4500
  Fax 617-929-4538
  E-mail: library@kennedy.nara.gov
  TTY 617-929-4523
  The Kennedy Library and Museum are located on Columbia Point in Boston, close to I-93
  The museum is open daily, 9:00 A.M.–5:00 P.M., except Thanksgiving Day, Christmas Day, and New Year's Day
  Call for current admission fees to the museum

- Richard Nixon Library & Birthplace
  18001 Yorba Linda Boulevard
  Yorba Linda, CA 92886
  714-993-3393
  Fax 714-528-0544
  Open daily, 10 A.M.–5 P.M.; Sundays, 11 a.m– 5 P.M., except Thanksgiving
    Day and Christmas Day
  Admission: Adults age 12 and above $5.95, children age 8 to 11 $2.00,
    children age 7 and below free, seniors age 62 and above $3.95, active
    military $4.95

- Ronald W. Reagan Presidential Library and Museum
  40 Presidential Drive
  Simi Valley, CA 93065-0666
  800-410-8354
  fax 805-522-9621
  E-mail: library@reagan.nara.gov
  Open Monday through Sunday, 10 A.M.–5 P.M.
  Admission: Adults $5, seniors $3, children 15 and under free

- Franklin D. Roosevelt Library and Museum
  511 Albany Post Road
  Hyde Park, NY 12538
  914-229-8114
  Fax 914-229-0872
  E-mail: library@roosevelt.nara.gov
  For tourist information only, call 800-FDR VISIT (800-337-8474)
  Open daily, 9 A.M.–5 P.M., except New Year's Day, Thanksgiving Day, and
    Christmas Day. Hours subject to change
  Call for current admission fees
  The Franklin D. Roosevelt Library and Museum is on the eastern shore
    of the Hudson River, four miles north of Poughkeepsie, midway
    between New York City and Albany

- Harry S. Truman Library
  500 West U.S. Highway 24
  Independence, MO 64050-1798
  24-hour information line 816-833-1225
  Administrative offices 816-833-1400; fax 816-833-4368
  E-mail: library@truman.nara.gov
  Web site: www.trumanlibrary.org

Open Monday through Saturday, 9 A.M.–5 P.M., until 9 P.M. on Thursdays; Sunday, 12 noon–5 P.M.

Admission: Adults $5.00, senior citizens $4.50, ages 6–18 $3.00, children under 6 free

Research room hours: Monday through Friday, 8:45 A.M.–4:45 P.M.

Itinerary of Our Colorado Trip

We felt that the pace of our 25-day itinerary was comfortable. We tried to keep our travel mileage under 400 miles a day. In addition, we have found that the body and mind seem to function better if there are some "stop and stay" days during a traveling vacation—for example, travel two or three full days and then stay in one place for two overnights or have a short travel day to the next overnight.

Day 1   Met the Graybeals and headed out
Arrived Spring Valley Campground, Cambridge, Ohio
Ate Paul's birthday cake in our motorhome with the Graybeals

Day 2   Lunched with friends in Columbus, Ohio
Visited I-70 Antique Mall, Springfield, Ohio
Arrived Cloverdale RV Park, Cloverdale, Indiana

Day 3   Saw flooding and brimming rivers during day's drive
Arrived Trailside Campers Inn of Kansas City, Grain Valley, Missouri

Day 4   Visited Truman Library and Museum, Independence, Missouri
Left Grain Valley, Missouri
Arrived Covered Wagon RV Park, Abilene, Kansas
Visited Museum of Telephony
Ate dinner at Kirby House, Abilene

Day 5   Toured Eisenhower Center, Abilene, Kansas
Left Abilene
Saw commencement processional at McPherson College
Arrived Gunsmoke Campground, Dodge City, Kansas

Day 6   Toured Old Dodge City Museum
         Left Gunsmoke Campground
         Arrived KOA Pueblo, Colorado

Day 7   Visited United States Air Force Academy
         Drove in Garden of Gods
         Visited Glen Eyrie and Miramont Castle Museum

Day 8   Crossed Royal Gorge Bridge
         Visited Cripple Creek
         Toured Van Briggle Pottery

Day 9   Spent morning in motorhome
         Visited Seven Falls
         Lunched at Broadmoor Hotel
         Toured ProRodeo Hall of Fame and Museum of the American
            Cowboy

Day 10   Left Pueblo, Colorado
         Arrived Alpen Rose RV Park, Durango, Colorado

Day 11   Bought tickets for Durango-Silverton Narrow Gauge Railroad
         Toured Mesa Verde National Park, Cliff Palace
         Shopped at Notah-Dineh, Cortez, Colorado

Day 12   Rode Durango-Silverton Narrow Gauge Railroad
         Lunched in Silverton
         Did laundry at campground

Day 13   Memorial Day Holiday
         Left Alpen Rose RV Park, Durango, Colorado
         Got stuck in snowstorm in San Juan Mountains
         Drove Million Dollar Highway
         Arrived Big J RV Park, Grand Junction, Colorado

Day 14   Left Big J RV Park, Grand Junction, Colorado
         Frolicked in Glenwood Hot Springs, Colorado
         Arrived Prospect RV Park & Campground, Wheat Ridge,
            Colorado

Day 15   Free day

Day 16 Toured United States Mint and Molly Brown House Museum
Visited Camp Colorado, Sedalia, Colorado

Day 17 Visited Estes Park, Colorado
Drove into Rocky Mountain National Park

Day 18 Toured Denver Museum of Natural History

Day 19 Left Prospect RV Park & Campground, Wheat Ridge, Colorado
Arrived KOA Denver East, Strasburg, Colorado
Visited Denver International Airport

Day 20 Left KOA Denver East, Strasburg, Colorado
Saw Pikes Peak in distance
Arrived Triple J Campground, Russell, Kansas

Day 21 Left Triple J Campground, Russell, Kansas
Arrived Shoemaker's RV Campground, Macon, Missouri

Day 22 Left 7:50 A.M. Shoemaker's RV Park, Macon, Missouri
Arrived Steamboat Bend Shopping Center, Hannibal, Missouri
Toured Mark Twain Home and Museum
Arrived 1:35 P.M. Mr. Lincoln's Campground, Springfield, Illinois
Visited Lincoln Home, Springfield, Illinois

Day 23 Left Mr. Lincoln's Campground, Springfield, Illinois
Arrived Enon Beach Campground, Springfield, Ohio

Day 24 Left Enon Beach Campground, Springfield, Ohio
Arrived Friendship Village Campground and RV Park, Bedford,
Pennsylvania

Day 25 Left Friendship Village Campground and RV Park, Bedford,
Pennsylvania
Arrived home

Campgrounds on Our Colorado Trip Itinerary

These are the campgrounds where the Graybeals, Paul, and I stayed as we traveled to Colorado and back from Maryland. They are listed in chronological order.

Ohio
- Spring Valley Campground, 8000 Dozer Road, Cambridge, OH 43725. Phone: 614-439-9291.

Indiana
- Cloverdale RV Park, 2789 E. County Rd. 800 S., Cloverdale, IN 46120. Phone: 765-795-3294; e-mail: cdalervp@ccrtc.com.

Missouri
- Trailside Campers Inn of Kansas City, 1000 R.D. Mize Road, Grain Valley, MO 64029. Phone: 1-800-748-7729.

Kansas
- Covered Wagon RV Park, 803 South Buckeye, Abilene, KS 64710. Phone: 913-263-2343.
- Gunsmoke Campground, West Highway 50, Dodge City, KS 67801. Phone: 1-800-789-8247.

Colorado
- KOA Pueblo, 4131 I-25 North, Pueblo, CO 81008. Phone: 719-542- 2273.
- Alpen Rose RV Park, 27847 Highway 550 North, Durango, CO 81301. Phone: 970-247-5540; fax: 970-259-8938.
- Big J RV Park, 2819 Highway 50, Grand Junction, CO 81503. Phone: 970-242-2527.
- Prospect RV Park & Campground, 11600 W. 44th Avenue, Wheat Ridge, CO 80033. Phone: 800-344-5702.
- KOA Denver East Kampground, Box 597, I-70 Exit 310, Strasburg, CO 80136. Phone: 303-622-9274; fax: 303-622-9274.

Kansas
- Triple J Campground, 187 Edwards, Russell, KS 67665. Phone: 913- 483-4826.

Missouri
- Shoemaker's RV Park, Highway 36, Box 6, Bevier, MO 63532 (listed in campground directory under Macon, Missouri). Phone: 800-530-5923.

Illinois
- Mr. Lincoln's Campground, 3045 Stanton Avenue, Springfield, IL 62703. Phone: 217-529-8206: fax 217-529-6725; e-mail: mlrv@fgi.net.

Ohio
- Enon Beach Campground, 2401 Enon Road, Springfield, OH 45502. Phone: 513-882-6431.

Pennsylvania
- Friendship Village Campground and RV Park, 548 Friendship Village, Bedford, PA 15522. Phone: 800-992-3528; fax: 814-623-3076; e-mail: camping@nb.net.

Travel Checklist

You will find a variety of checklists offered in the RV world, such as in RV magazines and from RV sales and service centers. The checklist that follows is the one Paul and I actually use. I set it up originally when we first bought our motorhome. Over the succeeding 11 years I've refined it as I learned what we would and would not need on the road. You will want to add those items unique to your special needs, interests, and destinations, of course.

The checklists—one for Paul and one for me—include what we normally try to keep in stock in the motorhome as well as reminders of what items to take along on each excursion. Paul and I each scan our lists before heading out. They are long lists, but we have learned to scan them quickly because we know which items are already on board and which details have been taken care of. Using the checklist gives us the satisfaction of knowing that when we pull out of the driveway we have on board what we will need (or know what we have to get along the way) and that our affairs at home are handled.

Motorhome Checklist—Bernice

Kitchen and Dining Area Supplies and Equipment
Place settings for eight—microwavable, nonbreakable dishes
Silverware for four
Acrylic tumblers
Plastic knives, forks, spoons
Plastic cereal bowls
Paper plates
Paper cups
Paper napkins
Placemats for eight
Tablecloth and seat covers for picnic table
Paper towels (two rolls for kitchen, one roll for windshield)
Bottle opener
Spatula
Butcher knife

Paring knife
Serrated-edge knife
Sieve spoon
Measuring spoons
Measuring cups
Ice cream dipper
Dish cloth
Tea towels (four)
Hand towels, Turkish (four)
Cleansing/scouring powder
Dishwashing liquid
Liquid hand soap
Laundry detergent
Spot-and-stain remover
Fabric softener sheets
Quart plastic pitcher
Electric can opener
Windowpane cleaning liquid spray
Waxed paper—one roll
Plastic wrap—one roll
Aluminum foil—one roll
Sandwich plastic bags
Freezer plastic bags
Trash bags to line wastebasket
Clothespins (twelve)
Clothesline
Matches
Candles for light
Candles for birthday cakes
Plastic water bucket, one- or two-gallon size
Plastic wash basin
Steel wool pads
Plastic scrubber for removing dried-on foods from cookware
Hot mats (four)
Oven mitts (two)
Fly swatter
Tape measure
Pen flashlight
Wastebasket
Pens
Pencil with eraser

Eraser
Pencil sharpener (hand-held)
Memo pad for writing grocery lists
Scissors
Needle
Thimble
Sewing thread

Bathroom Supplies and Equipment
Prescription medicines
Bathroom tissue
Chemical to deodorize holding tank
Baking soda for toilet (alternative for chemical above)
Toilet-bowl brush
Facial tissues (at least three boxes—one each for bath, bedroom, passenger
    seat)
Headache tablets
Antiseptic
Self-stick bandages
Cough drops
Upset stomach liquid or tablets
Calcium tablets
Enema preparation
Fever thermometer
Bath powder
Moleskin
Cotton tips
Petroleum jelly
Lip balm
Rubbing alcohol
Shampoo
Hair dryer (electric)
Extension cord
Insect repellent
Toothbrush
Toothpaste
Dental floss
Razor
Hair pick
Comb
Spring clips for hair (four)
Shower cap

Deodorant
Moisturizing cream
Foundation liquid
Rouge
Makeup brushes
Lipstick
Hair spray
Nail clippers
Nail file
Nail polish
Nail polish remover
Magnifying mirror
Tweezers
Nail scissors
Wash cloths (four)
Hand towels (four)
Body towels (four)

Bedroom Supplies and Equipment
Pillows (two)
Sheets (two queen size)
Thermal blanket (one queen size)
Thermal bedspread (one queen size)
Mattress cover (one queen size)
Goose-down comforter (store in overhead cabinet until needed)
Bible
Dictionary
Resource books for hobbies such as writing, crafts

Wardrobe Accessories and Equipment
Hangers in each closet (four)
Hats
Lightweight boots that go over shoes
Winter boots
Umbrellas
Bathrobe
Laundry bag

Where we are going determines what other clothes we take, such as blouses, shirts, pants, skirts, coats, jackets, sweaters, shorts, vests, and shoes. I always take a raincoat and plastic rain cap. We also add everyday items such as underwear, socks, hose, shoes, pajamas, bedroom slippers, and jewelry.

Handbag Items

I use a handbag large enough to hold my camera if necessary and add the following:

House keys

Motorhome keys

Car keys

Credit card (as few as possible—carrying only one is recommend by safety experts)

Plastic rain cap

Hair care instructions for hair stylists en route

Wallet with driver's license

Living Room Supplies and Equipment

Sofa pillows (two)

Afghan

Stationery

Tablets of lined paper

Games (playing cards and others)

Magazines

Home telephone directory

Address book

Stamps (for both first-class letters and postcards)

Broom for sweeping scatter rug and awning outside

Whisk broom

Journal

Trip log

Files from the house as relevant

Laptop computer

Printer that works with computer

Paper and envelopes for printer

Driving Area Supplies and Equipment

Sunglasses

Calculator

Audio cassette tapes

Cellular telephone

Binoculars

Map of each state we'll be going through

Atlas

Campground directory (to locate campgrounds)

Reservation confirmations or information

Tour books

Magnifying glass
Proof of vehicle insurance

To Do Before Leaving Home

Turn on refrigerator a few days before leaving to be sure it works, to begin freezing ice cubes, and to load frozen foods.

Load electric toaster if we're going on a long journey and we think we'll want toasted bread.

Leave license plate number of RV with appropriate person.

Leave telephone numbers and addresses of stops en route with appropriate person.

Leave obituary file in obvious place and be sure appropriate person has a house key and knows location of important papers. (The obituary file contains our instructions in the event of death.)

Make arrangements for mail: (1) use mail forwarding service or (2) ask appropriate person to handle mail while we are away or (3) arrange with post office to forward or hold mail.

Get maps and tour books as needed and place in passenger seat area.

Call neighbors on either side of house and perhaps across the street to let them know our departure and return dates. Also notify police of these dates.

Get groceries or load RV from what we have on hand. We usually follow our normal eating patterns when on the road: (1) breakfast consists of cereal, fruit, and skim milk; (2) lunch consists of a sandwich, fruit, and dessert; and (3) dinner consists of a meat, two vegetables, fruit, bread, and dessert. For snacks on the road, we choose pretzels and graham crackers. The following is our typical grocery list:

    Milk
    Bananas
    Cereal
    Peanut butter
    Canned fruit
    Canned soups
    Jelly
    Canned vegetables (small cans)
    Puddings in individual servings
    Cranberry juice
    Sodas in individual bottles with screw caps
    Graham crackers
    Soda crackers
    Frozen travel dinners
    Frozen meats

Ice cream
Bread or rolls
Margarine or butter
Vegetable oil cooking spray
Salt—can keep on board
Sugar—can keep on board
Flour
Eggs
Coffee for guests
Granola bars
Individual cakes or cookies

Motorhome Checklist—Paul

Bathroom Supplies and Equipment
Toothbrush
Toothpaste
Razor
Shaving cream
aftershave lotion
Comb
Prescription medicines

Wardrobe Accessories and Equipment
Bathrobe
Coveralls
Yellow slicker
Baseball caps
Short-sleeved shirts
Long-sleeved shirts
Jeans
Sport trousers
Sport shorts
Sweaters
Tee shirts
Shorts
Swim trunks
Socks
Handkerchiefs
Belts
Shoes
Hiking boots

Driving Area Supplies and Equipment
House keys
Motorhome keys
Credit and debit cards
Senior and campground membership cards
Registration card for motorhome
Flashlight with spare batteries
Sunglasses
Swiss army knife

Living Room Area
Files from house we want to take along
Magazines from house we want to take along

Outside Storage Supplies and Equipment
Folding lawn chairs (two)
Mud rug for outside entrance steps to motorhome
Antifreeze for water system
Applicable tools such as
    flat and Phillips-head screwdrivers
    pliers
    wrenches
    socket wrenches and socket set
    a spark plug socket wrench
    an inexpensive electric test light or voltmeter to diagnose electrical dif-
        ficulties
    quality jumper cables
Critical items such as
    tire-changing equipment
    extra drive belts for the engine
    extra coolant for chassis engine
    extra 12-volt fuses for both coach and chassis systems
    fuel filters appropriate for the RV
    spare top and bottom radiator hoses
    a few feet of extra heater hose
    electrical wire and crimp-on terminals
    rolls of duct and electrical tape
    a few clean rags
    flares
    reflective warning signs

To Do Before Leaving Home
Check on gasoline for motorhome and tow car—fill tanks as needed

Check on propane gas

Obtain supply of oil for motorhome engine

Obtain supply of oil for tow car engine

Stop newspaper

Get cash in $20 bills

Make sure funds are in account for debit card

Pay ahead the following:

    house and car insurance

    gasoline service bill

    gas and electric bill

    telephone bill

    fuel oil bill

Lubricate chassis

Change oil and oil filter of motorhome engine and refill, if necessary

Change transmission oil and filter and refill, if necessary

Check auxiliary generator to be sure it operates and check oil level and change as noted in manual

Check front wheel bearings and brake pads

Check radiator

Check furnace to be sure it works properly

Check water heater to be sure it works properly

Check tires (spare also)

Check all lights outside and inside to be sure they work

Check batteries

Take along any additional specialty tools that might be needed

Take along books and literature that may be needed for maintenance or repair

Check power-steering fluid

Check brake fluid

If going to another country, follow instructions of tour company

Get proof of vehicle coverage from RV insurance provider

Glossary

Black water. Waste (sewage) from the toilet that is flushed into a black water holding tank, usually located beneath the main floor of the RV.

Boondocking. Camping in an RV without benefit of electricity, fresh water, and sewer utilities. Boondockers should follow the rules of courtesy and the local laws about where to camp. The term came originally from people who parked (or docked) out in the "boonies" (boondocks— remote rural areas, back country, backwoods, sticks) where there were no hookups or other luxuries such as swimming pools.

Cabover. That part of the RV's body that extends over the cab and is used for a bedroom or storage. This RV is known as a Type C or Class C motorhome.

Campfire. A gathering around an outdoor fire for warmth, to enjoy roasting or toasting food, and for sociability.

Campground. A place to camp, usually with designated sites for RVs or tents. A campground may be private or public and usually has a user fee. It also usually has a host, manager, or owner who administers the policies or rules of the campground.

Campground directory. A listing of available campgrounds with descriptions of facilities available and directions for finding them.

Campground association. An organization of independent campground owners or of campground chains, such as the National Association of RV Parks & Campgrounds (ARVC).

Camping club. An organization established to provide certain benefits related to RVing for its members. Some camping clubs are for people with a variety of RVs, some are for owners of specific brands of RVs.

Camping group. A group of RVers who get together for camping weekends or trips and social events on an informal basis, with a volunteer wagonmaster who makes reservations for campgrounds, collects deposits, and arranges social events.

Caravan tour. A group of travelers using a specific mode of transportation such as RVs to explore a selected area of the country. Commercial caravan tours may run from 10 days to two months and are hosted by a tour company that usually provides a wagonmaster.

Checklist. A list of items or tasks used by RVers to be sure they have all items necessary on board and have completed necessary tasks.

Coach. Another name for a motorhome.

Conversion vehicle. A vehicle such as a van, truck, or sport-utility vehicle, manufactured by an automaker and then modified by a company that specializes in customizing vehicles. The modifications may include sofas, windows, carpeting, paneling, seats, and accessories.

Docking. Parking an RV at a place for overnight or longer.

Drop-off. A very steep descent alongside a road or highway.

Dry camping. Another name for boondocking. See Boondocking.

Dumping. To empty out, as in draining the holding tanks of an RV. Dumping is accomplished by removing the outlet safety cap and attaching a flexible hose to the outlet located on the RV holding tanks, inserting the opposite end of the flexible hose into a dumping station inlet pipe, usually located in a concrete sewer opening. See Holding tanks.

Dump station. Usually a concrete pad with an inlet opening connected to an underground sewage system at a campground or other facility offering dumping service to RV travelers.

Fifth-wheel trailer. Similar to a travel trailer except that its construction lends itself to a bi-level floor plan. It is normally pulled by a pickup-truck-style vehicle equipped with a fifth-wheel hitch fastened to the bed of a truck.

Folding camping trailer. A camping unit on wheels with collapsible walls that fold inward so that it can be towed by a car, van, or truck. Also known as a pop-up.

Fresh water. Water suitable for human consumption.

Full-timing. Living in one's RV all year long. These RVers are known as full-timers.

Galley. The kitchen of an RV.

Gray water. Used water that drains from the kitchen and bathroom sinks and the shower into a holding tank, called a gray water holding tank, that is located under the main floor of the RV.

Holding tanks. Tanks located on the RV, normally on the underside, that store fresh water, gray water, and black water. See Black water and Gray water.

Hooking up. Connecting the RV to a supply of electricity and water and to the sewer receptacle at a campground or other site.

KOA. Kampgrounds of America, a franchise chain of RV parks in North America that offers camping facilities to vacationers and overnighters.

LP gas. See Propane.

Mobile home. A large house trailer designed to stay in one place that can only be moved by the proper towing vehicle. Usually 10 or 12 feet in width. It is not to be confused with a motorhome.

Monitor panel. A panel usually with lights and switches for checking the battery charge, space in waste tanks, LP gas, amount of fresh water in that tank, water pump operation, and other systems.

Motorhome. A self-propelled vehicle on wheels that serves as both transportation and home. It is built on a specially designed chassis and includes holding tanks and electrical, water, and sewage hookup connections. It provides complete living facilities. There are three types or classes of motorhomes: Type A or Class A looks similar to a bus, Type B or Class B is a van camper, and Type C or Class C is known as a cabover.

Park. Another name for a campground. See Campground. Also, an area of land set aside by a city, state, or nation, usually in its mostly natural state, equipped with facilities for rest and recreation for the public to enjoy.

Parking. Docking; locating an RV in a site at a campground or other similar facility.

Park-model trailer. A spin-off of a recreational vehicle and a mobile home. It is a maximum of 8½ feet wide and 40 feet long, which is within the towability limits for an RV and may be parked in an RV park. Park-models have many options that movable RVs do not, such as regular appliances and furniture instead of built-ins. People who winter in one place other than their home location often opt for a park-model for their temporary living quarters.

Potluck. A group meal to which participants bring various foods to be shared.

Propane. Also known as LP gas. A colorless, flammable, liquefied petroleum gas that provides fuel to the furnace, refrigerator, water heater, and stovetop range in RVs. Most campgrounds offer this product. Although our LP gas tank holds 21.8 gallons, it is never filled more than 80 percent because the liquefied gas requires space to vaporize before leaving the tank.

Pull-through or pull-through site. These sites allow the driver of an RV to pull into the space, hook up, camp, and depart by simply pulling ahead onto a campground road. RV drivers appreciate them because they do not require backing into a space or site. Sometimes they are called drive-throughs.

RV or recreational vehicle. A vehicle used for recreational purposes, such as camping, and usually equipped with living facilities. An RV can be a motorhome, fifth-wheel travel trailer, travel trailer, folding camping trailer, truck camper, or conversion vehicle. See individual listings of RV types.

Resort. A place where people go to relax, rest, and enjoy recreation facilities. A camping resort usually has more than the usual campground amenities, such as whirlpools, golf courses, craft rooms, planned social events, tennis courts, and others.

Rig. Another name for a recreational vehicle.

Self-contained. An RV that has holding tanks for the gray water (bath and dish water) and for the black water (sewage).

Tailgunner. A person designated to assist mainly with mechanical problems of RVs during a caravan tour.

Tow car. A vehicle such as an automobile, van, or pickup truck that either pulls or is pulled by an RV. Motorhomes often pull small cars or trucks behind them for use for short errands or sightseeing in cities.

Travel trailer. A hard-sided unit on wheels towed by an automobile, van, or truck that usually contains living quarters. It is hitched to the towing vehicle.

Truck camper. A hard-sided portable unit of living quarters designed to be mounted on the bed or chassis of a pickup truck.

Unhooking. Disconnecting the electric cord from the campground outlet and storing the cord in its compartment in the RV, disconnecting the water hose from the campground faucet and storing the hose in its compartment in the RV, and disconnecting and stowing the black water hose. See Dumping.

Unit. Another name for a recreational vehicle.

Van camper. A panel-type vehicle that includes at least two of the following conveniences: kitchen, sleeping, and toilet facilities. The RV manufacturer of this vehicle must also include 120-volt hookup and city water hookup connections, and fresh water storage. This type of RV is known as a Type B or Class B motorhome.

Wagonmaster. A leader, either hired or chosen, who guides a caravan of recreational vehicles on a trip. The wagonmaster usually makes advance reservations for campgrounds, shows, cruises, sightseeing, and group meals.

Index